"Don't make things worse!"

Hansen whined with a stutter, feeling he was losing control.

Hysterical, the woman kept slapping him, screaming that he was going to kill her.

Finally, Hansen released his grip, allowing his prey to stumble away as fast as she could.

The woman could see the sandbar and the river beyond as she reached the edge of the woods. The .223 bullet burst her heart before the sound of the rifle shot reached her ear . . . .

FAIR GAME

Bernard DuClos

ST. MARTIN'S PAPERBACKS

ISBN: 0-312-92905-6

Printed in the United States of America

For *all* the victims

Acknowledgments

Many people helped me in various ways during my work to complete this book, and I'm grateful to them, one and all. A particular "thank you" to those who gave their time and shared their personal, sometimes painful recollections which enabled me to tell the story of *Fair Game;* several of those people have not only my thanks, but also my admiration and respect. And I want to express my appreciation to the Minnesota Coalition of Sexual Assault Services for the use of its book and film library.

Also, a special thanks to my agent, Jack Caravela, and Charlie Spicer and his staff at St. Martin's for their guidance and enthusiasm.

BERNARD DU CLOS

Author's Note

Fair Game is based on police and court records (1961–84), transcriptions of interviews (1983–84), and my own interviews with persons connected to the Robert Hansen case. I have re-created a few scenes and some dialogue to tell the story, using my research as my guide.

"Gloria Deacon" is a pseudonym for Robert Hansen's second wife; his children's first names aren't mentioned, nor is the name of his first wife.

"Barbara Fields" is a pseudonym at the victim's request.

Prologue

Rain and fog enveloped Alaska's Chugach Range on August 10, 1971, making its slopes treacherous for opening day hunters who stalked the Dall sheep. Two Anchorage bow hunters, Robert Hansen and John Sumrall, were about thirty miles into the mountains. They'd completed the first twelve miles in an all-terrain vehicle, set up a base camp, and with supplies and bows and arrows slung on their backs, packed in on foot through wind, rain, choking underbrush, swift streams, and around glacial moraines.

Strong summer winds had powdered the Chugach to an ashen hue with a new layer of glacial silt, which was now dark and slippery from the rain. To the sound of their own deep breathing, the hunters moved deliberately upward through the mist. If they slipped and struck a shin or knee on a rock, there'd be no acknowledgment. Perhaps later they'd notice the bruise.

The only gentlemanly aspect of hunting in Alaska is that it's expensive. With trophies and meat—and sometimes without—the hunters return to their camp or home exhausted, dirty, and occasionally with an injury. Once in a while they don't return at all. When the slopes are steep and slick with rain, some hunters will hold back or go home. But not Robert Hansen; he was after his ram.

The bag limit for the Chugach was one ram with a three-quarter horn curl or larger. Sheep horns grow from year to year, not shed like the antlers of a deer or moose, so a three-quarter curl means a four- or five-year-old sheep; a full curl indicates a ram is at least seven. Hansen had watched one particular animal all summer, a wise old hoofer whose curl was well beyond full.

According to Asian lore, the ram's horns could be ground into an aphrodisiac that would enhance sexual power. But to Hansen, the mammoth curl of the sheep he stalked symbolized a formidable adversary, a trophy ram whose head could hang on the wall of his den to validate his skills as a hunter. He already held the number-three position in the Pope and Young records for Dall sheep taken by a bow, and felt this ram could give him the top spot, the world record.

On many weekends Hansen had trekked into the Chugach to study the sheep's habits and let it get used to having him around. He'd been within a hundred yards of the animal a dozen times, but today he wanted to get within thirty-five yards to assure a clean kill with his bow.

The men saw the white cape at the same time and froze as the magnificent curl came up through the mist. It was the trophy ram, panning its surroundings as it chewed.

The ram lowered its head again to graze.

Hansen and Sumrall slid out of their packs. Hansen nocked an arrow.

There were other sheep, but the ram was between them and the hunters. Hansen motioned to Sumrall that he was going in closer. Inch by inch, stopping whenever the curl came up, Hansen moved to within twenty-five yards of the animal.

He stood erect and raised his bow, aiming for the vitals cavity just in back of the ram's shoulder. Hansen let the arrow fly; it disappeared into the white cape. The sheep jerked at the impact, then bolted out of sight around a butte.

"Looked like a good lung shot, Bob," Sumrall said as the two men scrambled toward the spot where the ram had been standing. The other sheep had scattered.

"J-John, I'll go this way, you g-go over there. . . ." Hansen stuttered when he got excited.

"Wait Bob, here's the arrow." Sumrall handed it to Hansen. "Went clean through."

Robert felt the arrow's fletching. It was wet and warm with blood. "He c-can't have gone far."

The fog had become more dense, and it continued to thicken after the two men split up to look for the ram. The rocky slopes melted in the mist; everything looked the same, making the search almost impossible. Finally, after two hours . . .

"Bob, over here! I almost tripped over him."

The ram had fallen between some boulders just sixty yards from where he'd been shot.

Hansen ran up and fell to his knees by the white carcass. What had been untouchable was now his to handle—he turned the lifeless head and its curl one way, then another.

"Bob, he's a beaut . . . a real fireplace ram."

"Y-Yeah. Well, John, we'd better get to it."

The rest of the daylight was spent taking pictures, caping—or skinning—the sheep and boning its meat. An official measurement of the curl for the record book would have to wait sixty days to allow the trophy to dry, but the men took a quick measure before heading down the slope.

"Bob, looks like you're gonna pack out a world record on your back," Sumrall said. "What'ya going after next?"

Just over three months later, Robert Hansen put a gun to the head of an eighteen-year-old woman and began leaving the trail of a stalk that made him the most prolific serial rapist and murderer in Alaska's history. For twelve years he victimized women in the Anchorage area, taking over twenty to their executions in the wilderness, several in his private plane.

Like Hansen the big-game hunter, Robert Hansen the murderer was methodical and tenacious, acting with a treacherous guile to snare his female prey. The fact that he didn't use a bow and arrow in this aberrant hunt seems to underline the difference he perceived between his trophy animals and human victims. With the bow, he hunted the cunning survivor; with a gun, he stalked the vulnerable, the "wounded."

Early on in his deadly rampage, Hansen designated his hunting grounds to be Anchorage's "tenderloin" district, an area that burgeoned during the heyday of the Alaskan pipeline boom, where many women driven by a hard-knocks life opted to work its streets and topless bars, sometimes on the end of a leash held by the Mafia or Hell's Angels. From their numbers, Hansen sought out the most naive, isolated, and desperate, knowing that if one of them did accuse him of rape, it would be the word of a "respectable business and family man" against that of a "woman of the streets." And when they disappeared, the chances were that no one would notice or care.

In 1984, when Robert Hansen finally answered for his crimes, the sentencing judge called the case before him "an indictment of society." The court documents contained an incredible history, part of a tragic story in which society and the judicial system had made Robert Hansen's victims *fair game*.

I

Tracks,

Chapter 1

Anchorage, April 24, 1983

In the basement of the Great Alaskan Bush Company, a topless-bottomless bar at 531 Fifth Avenue, floor manager Janice Scherpereel put on her coat and walked up the stairs, ascending into a darkness fragmented by pulsing light and pounding music. She paused.

Petite and attractive Paula Goulding was dancing on the stage, a "walk-in" whom Scherpereel had hired just a week before. The thirty-year-old Goulding had told her she'd left her secretarial job in Fairbanks to come down and earn more money as a dancer. The woman's good looks and eagerness had outweighed her inexperience and the unworldly air about her.

Now the floor manager was surprised to see Goulding slowly working the G-string down her wriggling thighs, going for the big tips already. Scherpereel knew she should give up trying to figure out what the women in her charge might do, whether they'd been sent by the Seattle mob, hopped off the back of a motorcycle, or just showed up out of the blue like Paula did. They all wanted or needed money for one reason or another; that's what brought them to the bars of Anchorage's tenderloin district.

Naked, Goulding finished her dance set and began to gather up the money scattered over the stage. Scherpereel headed for the door, her movement followed by *a hunter's eyes* staring through a pair of eyeglasses from a dark corner of the bar.

The person behind the stalking gaze knew who the floor manager was. When the door closed behind her, his eyes went back to the stage and Paula Goulding. She was new.

The man removed his glasses, finished the now warm beer he'd been nursing for almost an hour, and got up from the table. His left hand slid into his pants pocket and around a large roll of bills as he stealthily worked his way toward the stage by the darkest route he could find.

The $300 and what it would buy was what Paula thought about as she waited at the shopping mall. Last night the guy had said he'd meet her around 11:45 that morning, that he'd be in a blue car. Just past noon Goulding heard a voice hail her from a green car. "O-Over here."

It was him all right, though now he was wearing glasses and the car was green, not blue. That didn't matter.

He got out and politely opened the passenger door for her.

In the daylight, Paula could see pockmarks on the man's face. He was scarred, but with his slight build and quiet demeanor, he seemed harmless.

She relaxed as the car wound through one-way streets and onto the Glenn Highway, heading toward the Muldoon section of Anchorage. Paula had no idea that she was now a character in a script that had been played out scores of times in the last twelve years, and that its ending—her fate—would depend on how she acted.

In Muldoon the man turned the vehicle into a deserted parking lot. Paula wasn't suspicious when his arm went up and rested behind her, and his fingers began to play with her soft blond hair, nor did she notice his left hand slipping under the seat.

Suddenly her head was jerked back, hairs straining at their roots, and she saw a pistol barrel pointing toward her as a snarling voice stuttered a warning.

"All right, now you'll do just what I say. I'm good at this . . . done it lots of times before."

The action of the gun clicked.

"Do we understand each other?"

Wide-eyed, in terror, the woman gave a jerking nod.

Goulding's captor forced her onto her knees on the floor of the front seat, then handcuffed her hands behind her back. In this confining position, she was helpless.

"Stay down and be quiet," he said. "We're going to my airplane."

Terrified, Paula remained silent as the car headed southwest, retracing its route on the Glenn Highway.

They turned into a driveway at the northeast corner of Merrill Field and followed a road flanked by rows of private airplanes. Pulling up next to a Super Cub, the passenger side of the vehicle almost brushed a wing strut. The plane was blue and white, the most common color for a bush plane, and the registration numbers painted on its tail were the smallest size that aviation regulations allowed.

There were people milling around the Polar Airways hangar fifty yards away, but no one paid attention to the man in the car. Merrill Field is one of the largest and busiest private-plane airstrips in the world, averaging a takeoff every thirty seconds. Consequently, like neighbors in a bustling city, pilots don't necessarily know the persons whose planes are parked near theirs, nor do they pay heed to the comings and goings of other pilots.

"Keep down and stay quiet . . . I have some things to do," the voice snarled above Paula's head.

Afraid to budge, she stayed cramped on the floor of the front seat while the man got out of the car and released his plane from its tie-downs. After a visual check of its tires, flaps, and tail, he opened the door of the airplane, then turned to assess the activity at the nearby hangar.

Getting back in the car, he spoke with a deliberate tone. "There are some people outside. I'm going to wait until they're gone . . . then we'll get on the plane. You won't cause any problem now, will you?"

With her head down, crouched in a fetal position on her knees, Paula managed a trembling plea: "Just don't hurt me! I won't make any trouble!"

When he determined the coast was clear, the man whisked his captive aboard the plane. She stumbled only once, the circulation returning to her legs.

The rear seat had been removed from the Super Cub; this sort of passenger was stowed like cargo. He forced her down behind the pilot's seat.

"Now, I have to move the car about fifteen feet. Don't try to get out of the plane, because I'll be watching you. I'd hate to have to put a bunch of bullet holes in the airplane shooting at you."

Stark fear kept Paula from blinking an eye while her captor moved his car, then climbed into the pilot seat. The motor started, and she felt the big 150 engine shake the little plane as it began a slow taxi.

Reaching for a radio mike, the man at the controls noted the registration numbers on the tail of another airplane. "Merrill tower, this is Super Cub V7144C"—the numbers of the other plane—"requesting clearance for takeoff, over?"

The tower gave him clearance for runway 6.

As the oversized engine jerked the plane forward, causing Paula to shift in her cramped position, she became aware of the smell of doughnuts. An odd, incongruous aroma, she'd smelled it in the car too. She thought it might be coming from her abductor's clothes.

Abruptly, Goulding's train of thought was broken when she spotted a rifle stashed in the cockpit. The gun had a long clip, like ones she'd seen in gangster movies. Its possible implications heightened her terror.

Paula was shifted again as the plane lifted off the runway. A steep climb took it to a thousand feet by the time it flew over the tower; no one could have made out its registration numbers from there had they tried.

The pilot banked his plane sharply to the north to head for the Knik River, and its cargo was pressed against the fuselage.

With the g force holding Paula's head tight against the wall of the plane, the engine noise was amplified in her ear and the vibrations shook her mind and body. Then, as her captor brought the plane out of its turn, there was the smell of doughnuts again. . . .

Chapter 2

Texas, the following week

To Junior, the only good part of the trips down from Anchorage was the frequent flyer mileage they accumulated. In the visiting hall of the coed "country club" Federal Correction Center in Fort Worth, Gilbert "Junior" Pauole knew he was on the spot. He sat across from the reputed head of Seattle's leading crime family, Frank "Papa" Colacurcio, who wore a sour look which was erasing the almost perpetual dime-store grin on Junior's dark and round thirty-six-year-old Polynesian face.

Pauole was part of a steady stream of regular monthly visitors Colacurcio received, one of several pornography and topless nightclub managers from Alaska and the Pacific Northwest who came to the prison to report on their business, delivering information to their boss which they couldn't entrust in a letter or telephone call.

On this trip he was bringing bad news; the Alaska Alcohol Beverage Control Board had just closed the Wild Cherry, one of the topless bars Pauole operated for Colacurcio in Anchorage. To make matters worse, the "take on the skim" for April had totaled in the low four figures for the Cherry and the Good Times Lounge, the other club he managed for the Colacurcio organization.

"Gil, those fucking numbers stink!" his boss growled. "They're the lousiest in the eight years we've been up in that cold shithouse." Colacurcio could remember months when the skim had run up in the six figures. "Damn! Things need to be done, and my ass is rotting in here on a tax conviction!"

Pauole didn't want to look into the sinister eyes behind the thick, dark-rimmed glasses, so he focused on one of the chins between Colacurcio's sixty-five-year-old face and Adam's apple.

"So what you're telling me is the numbers won't be up next month . . . they'll be even worse with the Cherry closed. Am I right?" The lines in Colacurcio's face puckered; he was in a slow burn.

"The money isn't around like it used to be, Frank. Oil prices . . . shit, it's ten dollars a barrel, used to be thirty. Guys don't have money. . . ."

Pauole slouched down, waiting for a reaction.

On the other side of the table Colacurcio's heavy bulk swelled and shifted, then a hand went up and smoothed a dyed, oily coiffure—the stroking of the hair seemed to deflate the threat in the body. He knew Junior was a bullshitter, an illiterate punk who couldn't write his own name but could talk the underwear off a nun. He'd taken Pauole under his wing ten years ago, when they were cellmates at Washington State's McNeil Island penitentiary—he was doing time for racketeering, and Pauole was in for felony theft in Hawaii. Colacurcio now sensed that their relationship was on a downhill grade. Word was that Junior had an expensive monkey on his back—a cocaine habit.

"I want those numbers up, Gil," he said, leaning toward the balding Pauole. "Squeeze the dancers more, if you have to."

"I can try," Junior said without enthusiasm, then sighed. "But Frank, there's that problem. Girls are still droppin' out of sight. Since one dancer turned up dead, a lot of them think a killer's behind the disappearances, and the girls are scared, Frank. It's getting harder to control them . . . they're talking to the cops a lot. I don't know what to do—"

A guard interrupted. "Colacurcio, you've got another visitor."

"Oh, yeah? Send him in," Colacurcio said to the guard. He gave Junior a sneering look. "Maybe the next guy will have good news for me. Okay, we're done."

Pauole got up from the chair.

"See you, Gil." The tone wasn't amicable.

"Yeah, sure, Frank."

Colacurcio watched the five-nine Pauole walk toward the door, then he called to him across the room. "Oh, Gil."

Junior stopped and turned around.

An overweening smirk covered the Mafia boss's face. "Get those numbers up, Junior."

Chapter 3

Sergeant Lyle Haugsven sat at his desk in the AST—Alaska State Troopers—station on Tudor Road in Anchorage, taking the kind of phone call he'd come to dread. On the line was the city police Missing Persons Unit, informing him that yet another woman had disappeared from Anchorage's tenderloin district.

Twenty-two-year-old Tereasa "Nicolle" Watson had, in fact, been missing since March 25, just over a month. Her roommate, Pat Hutchinson, had tried to report Nicolle missing that very next day, but was told by police that it was too soon to file a missing persons report. When she tried again the following day, she was told the same thing.

Discouraged, and trying to convince herself that maybe she was worrying needlessly, Hutchinson had let the matter drop and left for a vacation in California.

Down in Sacramento, her hometown as well as Watson's, she discovered that Nicolle's mother had lost contact with her daughter. Alarmed, Hutchinson went to the police as soon as she got back up to Alaska.

A tempered sadness dragged on Lyle Haugsven's square-jawed face as he listened to the Anchorage police officer on the phone. Working on the missing dancers case, he'd heard too many stories like this over the past eight months. He hadn't come to Alaska for this.

Born in Pelican Rapids, Minnesota, in 1942, Lyle had moved with his family to the Pacific Northwest when he was three. The Haugsvens eventually settled in Brewster, Washington, just forty miles southeast of the North Cascades National Park. It was the Cascades that created Lyle's love of the outdoors and wilderness —his summers as a teenager were spent working at different jobs in the park, then as a firefighter/smoke jumper during his college breaks. He logged ninety-nine parachute jumps before hanging up his silks. After earning a degree from Ohio State's University of the Americas, Lyle joined the U.S. Forest Service, and beginning in 1964, drew summer tours of duty in Alaska. In 1968 Lyle made the forty-ninth state his home, and joined the state troopers two years later.

Now, propping the receiver on one of his broad shoulders, Haugsven began taking notes of the conversation.

Tereasa Watson, known to her friends as Nicolle, had come up to Anchorage in January and gone to work at the Foxy Lady—"Touch of Honey" massage parlor and dating service. The five-foot-two, blue-eyed Nicolle was described as "pretty," wearing her blond hair short on top—feathered—and medium length on the sides.

Nicolle's friends knew she was blind in one eye; a stranger wouldn't notice it because her bad eye coordinated muscularly well with her good one. A rough lifestyle had left Watson with a bad kidney, and her teeth were in poor condition. Nicolle wore a false upper front tooth that seemed to fall out at the drop of a hat, and despite the urgings from her friends to quit or cut down, she chain-smoked Kool 100s.

Sergeant Haugsven bit at his lower lip as he listened, then shook his head slightly as he sighed and asked, "So what are the details of Watson's disappearance?"

On March 25 Nicolle had told her roommate she was going to meet a man at a restaurant called Flippers West. She described her date as "a real nice man" she'd met recently, who'd promised to pay her $300 if she'd have lunch and spend an hour or so with him. A friend dropped her off at the restaurant at two-thirty that afternoon, and Nicolle hadn't been seen or heard from since.

A $300 lunch date. Lyle had heard that scenario described before.

Taking the receiver off his shoulder and grasping it in his hand, the trooper sergeant said, "Look, I'll go to the Foxy Lady . . . they probably have a picture of her, a Polaroid at least. I'll swing by later to pick up your paper on the case."

Hanging up the phone, Lyle found himself wishing he was stationed up above the Arctic Circle again. During three years of patrolling 42,000 square miles of northern Alaska, he'd gotten to know the people in the dozen or so villages scattered up there, had shared some of their joys, not just the troubles. This was all grief. The missing dancers . . . Lyle came to feel he knew each of them just by talking to their friends, and in some cases their families.

What every homicide investigator tries to avoid when a case drags on or expands to more victims, is getting emotionally involved. It had already happened to Haugsven; he cared about the missing women—many of them were so young. The thought that they could all be dead, like Sherry Morrow, a missing dancer from the Wild Cherry whose body had been found last September along the Knik River, made him angry. Contributing to that anger was his feeling that outside the friends and families of the missing women, and some of the troopers investigating the cases, not too many people seemed to give a damn. And Haugsven loathed hearing any law officer or civilian referring to the missing women as "whores."

A year ago, when he'd been investigating white-collar crimes for the troopers' Criminal Investigation Bureau, everyone kept telling him, "Lyle, you need a few months in the CIB's homicide division to round out your experience," so he'd requested a short stint. But now he wondered just how long it was going to be. He knew he couldn't walk away from the missing dancers case.

Haugsven breathed deeply as he walked to the parking lot, looking around at the quintet of mountain ranges that cupped Cook Inlet and Anchorage in a horseshoe, separating them from the 500,000 square miles of Alaska on the other side. Almost half of the state's population was crammed into the 126 square miles of the Anchorage bowl. But that's where the state's best schools were, and Lyle and Gail Haugsven had three children—daughter Aimee and sons Lyle and Sean.

Reaching his unmarked car, the sergeant leaned against the vehicle for a few moments and thought about doing patrol out of Glennallen or up north out of Kotzebue. Then, giving the roof of the cruiser a slap, he got in and headed downtown.

Chapter 4

It was almost noon. In the Hansen Bakery, a few blocks from downtown Anchorage, a hand reached into the cash register and cleaned out the day's receipts, leaving just a little cash for change.

Robert Hansen stuffed the money into a doughnut bag, told his foreman and employees he'd see them tomorrow, and headed out to the parking lot.

As he slid behind the steering wheel of his Buick Century, his breathing became short and deep. Robert Hansen was starting to boil inside.

At the exit to the parking lot he looked down at the bag of cash on the seat and considered driving downtown. He wanted to, but it could be risky. Instead, he headed for the Muldoon section of Anchorage.

A few minutes later he pulled into the driveway of a gray, one-story ranch that sprawled on an acre lot among tall pines. The doughnut bag in his hand, he hurried into the house and down the stairs to the basement.

He paused in the doorway of a room where the noonday light crept through a small window, to ricochet off cold, dead eyes. *The hunter* was entering his den.

Slowly walking the periphery of the room, he touched the lifeless snouts of mountain sheep and goats—trophy mounts that symbolized his skills as a hunter . . . *his power!*

After lingering in the doorway again, he ran upstairs to the kitchen. Throwing the sack of money into an oak cupboard, he grabbed some paper towels and headed for the master bedroom.

Robert Hansen propped a pillow against the headboard of his bed, from behind which he pulled an aviation chart of the Anchorage bowl and adjoining Mat-Su Valley. Resting his head on the pillow, he unfolded the map, which was covered with several dark asterisks he'd drawn over the years.

Now he stared at the one he'd marked most recently—one of several clustered on the chart along the Knik River. Things hadn't gone very well nine days ago. . . .

He'd landed his Super Cub on a gray-pebbled sandbar two miles upriver from the new Glenn Highway bridge that spanned the Knik River. It was an area popular with moose hunters; Hansen liked it too. He'd brought a woman there the week before, got what he wanted, then flew her back to Anchorage. This time he'd had a terrified Paula Goulding in his aircraft.

Hansen taxied away from the river and parked the plane near a scrub-brush thicket. He killed the engine, then reached around the seat and removed the handcuffs from Paula's now-tender wrists.

"Don't do anything stupid," he told her, "or you'll regret it. Take ahold of the back of the seat and the window supports . . . you'll be able to get out that way."

Hansen put the handcuffs in his jacket pocket and stuffed a .22-caliber pistol under his belt as he climbed out of the cockpit. He turned to help Goulding step down.

Paula was able to glance across the wide breadth of the Knik River before she was yanked by the arm.

"This way. There's a meat shack in the woods . . . that's where we'll spend the day."

Her captor's words intensified her fear, and the woman dragged her feet to resist.

Suddenly, from upriver, there was the sound of an engine!

A bush plane came flying overhead and went into a lazy turn to circle back.

"Shit! The son of a bitch is going to land!" Hansen stuttered. He gave his victim a jerk and snarled, "If he does, don't say a goddamn word to him. If you raise hell, I'm going to shoot both of you. . . . *You* don't want to die, do you?"

"Oh, no, no!" Paula gasped.

"Good. Let's go."

Hansen pulled her into the woods toward the meat shack as the plane continued to circle over the river.

It was a crude structure, with a screen door held shut by a bent nail. When Hansen got her inside, Paula looked up and saw a long iron pipe suspended between two posts, running the length of the shack. She didn't know it was there for hanging moose meat, to protect a hunter's bounty from crawling bugs, but its looks had a sinister aspect that added to her terror.

Shoving his captive against one of the posts, Hansen handcuffed her hands behind her around the support. Paula gave a futile tug at the cuffs as he once again warned her to stay quiet, then hurried outside. He wanted his Mini-14; the .223-caliber rifle was still in the cockpit.

The plane had circled and made three passes. When Hansen reached his Super Cub, he looked up and waved as it flew over again. This time the pilot dipped his wings and continued on down the river.

Relieved, Hansen grabbed his rifle out of the plane and headed back to the meat shack, where his captive despairingly sank to her knees as she heard the sound of the airplane engine fade away.

Leaning the rifle against the outside of the building and putting his pistol down beside it, Hansen went in and uncuffed Paula.

Desperation and hysteria now overcame her submissive paralysis, and she jumped to her feet, slapping and screaming at her captor, "You're going to kill me!"

Hansen's denials didn't calm her down. Paula bolted free and ran out of the shack, her panic escalating when she heard the footsteps and panting growing louder behind her, then felt a hand grab her shoulder.

"It's cool!" Hansen swung the woman around and shook her. "No problem . . . the guy's gone," he said, almost pleading.

"No, you're going to kill me!" Paula shrieked, then broke away again and ran.

Robert got his rifle and went after her; he caught up and snagged her by the shirt; it ripped down the back as she stumbled to her knees.

"Don't make things worse!" he whined with a stutter, feeling he was losing control.

Hysterical, the woman kept slapping at him, screaming that he was going to kill her.

Hansen wasn't going to say any more. He released his grip, allowing his prey to stumble away as fast as she could.

Paula Goulding could see the sandbar and the river beyond as she reached the edge of the woods. The .223 bullet burst her heart before the sound of the rifle shot reached her ear. . . .

Now, several days later, Paula's killer folded the map he'd been looking at, fondling it briefly before stashing it back in its place behind the headboard of the bed.

He looked at the palm of his hand, which tingled slightly from the evaporation of residual semen that hadn't made it into the paper towel. The sliver was healed —he'd had to dig Goulding's grave with a rough board he ripped off the shack.

Hansen got off the bed and carried the paper towel laced with semen into the bathroom and flushed it down the toilet. Then he headed for the living room.

It had been a miserable week for Robert Hansen; it always was when "things didn't go right." Not that he felt any guilt or remorse for the killings; it was the fear of getting caught that worried him. Sometimes he fantasized that his house was surrounded by police cars—the cops corralling the killer.

And even when things went right, there was always his fear that something *could* go wrong at any minute. The oral sex he forced his victims to perform wasn't exciting him like it used to. The topless bars were closing, shrinking his hunting grounds and increasing the possibility that he'd be recognized, even though he used makeup and disguises on several of his "hunts" in the tenderloin district.

It was time for a change.

Going into the living room, Hansen stepped over his wife's poodle and around some toys to get to a stack of newspapers. The dog watched him hunt through the pile and pull out the classifieds from the Sunday *Anchorage Daily News*.

In the kitchen, he found a pencil and sat down at the table. He glanced again at the "Sunday Singles" blurbs—he'd read them carefully a few days before.

After studying the instructions for placing a singles ad, he surveyed the form provided on the page to compose one.

Smiling to himself, he began to write on the blank lines provided under "Here's my ad." A sentence on the form reminded the customer: "Remember, you'll get best results from describing YOURSELF fully."

Later that afternoon, Hansen drove to the *Daily News* offices and arranged to have the ad he'd composed run twice. He paid with cash he'd taken from the doughnut bag; he didn't want a canceled check betraying his activities to his wife.

The ad appeared in the paper's "Sunday Singles" on May 8 and 15. Robert indicated he was looking for a woman with whom "to share [a] sincere, honest attachment," one who had an active social life and enjoyed outdoor activities like beachcombing, fishing, camping and flying into the bush. His ad concluded, "Life is beautiful, much fuller if shared. [Send] Recent photo."

Chapter 5

When Alaska State Trooper Wayne Von Clasen was completing a degree program in geology at Western Washington State in Bellingham, he never dreamed that years later he'd be in a club named the Great Alaskan Bush Company giving a lecture on personal safety to a group of nude dancers.

"Realize that if you *do* prostitute yourself, you increase the chance for violence against your person by twentyfold. You protect your health with condoms, you protect your person with a Mace aerosol or whatever is handy." Von Clasen, a heavyset Paul Sorvino lookalike, knew some of the women probably carried knives and small caliber pistols—weapons illegal to conceal, but he stuck to the "do's."

"And when you leave work to walk home or to your vehicle, go in pairs. If you can't find a buddy, try to get a bouncer or doorman to accompany you. If you see a trooper in the club, ask him to escort you. *Don't* trust a customer or stranger . . . Any questions?"

After a few beats of silence, a tall, large, brown-haired woman stood up at her desk at the back of the room.

"Okay, girls, that's it. Next shift, you're up." Bush Company owner Edna Cox came up to talk to Von Clasen as the young dancers filed out of the room.

"Thanks for the talk. But I'm afraid we have another missing girl. A newcomer, danced here just a few days. No one has seen her for over two weeks. She was a walk-in, wasn't booked for the circuit. Didn't have a boyfriend as far as we know."

"Edna, let me use your desk and I'll take down the details. Give me her picture, if you have one. Can I use your phone for a second?"

Sergeant Lyle Haugsven put down the receiver and looked at the bulletin board behind his desk. Another name was going on it: PAULA GOULDING.

Two names were by themselves on the board, not part of the long column of "missing" that also included the name of Sherry Morrow, the dancer from the Wild Cherry whose body was found along the Knik River nine months before by moose hunters. The first was Eklutna Annie, a Jane Doe found in a shallow grave outside Anchorage in 1980—she'd been murdered in '79. The other, Joanne

Messina, was killed in May 1980, and her body found two months later in a gravel pit near Seward.

Morrow's killer had used a .223-caliber rifle. But Annie was killed with a knife, and Messina by two .22-caliber bullets. Though no common weapon linked the trio of homicides, the victims were all young and attractive women whose bodies were found in shallow graves.

Did the two names belong with the rest?

On May 25 Joe Majors, owner/operator of a topless bar called Murphy's Law, reported that one of his dancers, Angela Feddern, had been missing for almost three months. He realized that he probably should have notified the police sooner.

Young Feddern lived at the downtown Palace Hotel and split her time dancing at Murphy's Law and another club, the Arctic Fox. Occasionally she worked Fourth Avenue as a prostitute.

Majors said the last time he saw Angela was in late February, when he'd asked her one day if she'd be dancing that evening. She told him no, she was going to work "the Avenue" instead, and that she had a trick lined up for $300. The club manager recalled that Feddern said the guy was a doctor, very ugly, but carried a big roll of money.

When Angela Feddern's name went on Lyle Haugsven's bulletin board, the count of missing women stood at nine, with the common denominator among them being their working environs—Anchorage's downtown streets, topless bars, and massage parlors. The women who worked in the city's tenderloin district lived solitary lives on society's fringe, cloistered in downtown hotels and bound in a constricted lifestyle in which their makeup and worldly posturing was usually a mask to cover their own naiveté, vulnerability, or desperation. They were isolated from the mainstream in a sorority of street talk and street smarts where outsiders were generally viewed with suspicion, particularly law enforcement officers.

In some instances the mistrust hampered police investigations, as it had in the case of Andrea Altiery, whose name was on the troopers' bulletin board. For three months after she was reported missing in December '81, police thought they were investigating the disappearance of *Lisa* Altiery, her sister. The reason: when friend and roommate Royale Delcazza reported Altiery missing, she knew Andrea was carrying Lisa Altiery's IDs. (Lisa was a student attending the University of Hawaii, and not in Alaska.) Afraid that a hassle might develop for Andrea if police found her using her sister's identification, Delcazza played it safe and stuck with her roommate's charade—saying it was Lisa who had disappeared.

There were other confusions over who was who, because many women had the same or similar stage or street names. An officer might be told by a girl on the street, "Sure, I worked with a dancer named 'Pepper,' but I haven't seen her for quite a while." Then, proceeding with an investigation of "Pepper's" disappearance, the trooper might find out that there were three or four dancers in Anchorage clubs going by that same name.

Another problem was that some of the women seemed insensitive to the possibility that there could be a kidnapper-killer in their midst. Perhaps it was the harshness of their peripheral world, but many would think a disappearance might be related to the struggle between the factions—the mob, Hell's Angels, pimps—that wielded power over the clubs, bars, and streets. Maybe a missing friend had left on the back of a motorcycle, or a coworker had been booked into a topless bar in another state by her agency, Talents West, run by the Mafia in Seattle.

Sometimes dancers would have to face down intimidation if they decided to seek help in finding a friend who'd disappeared. The Futrell case was a poignant example.

Laura Fulton and Joy Stewart were very concerned when their roommate dropped out of sight. Lisa Futrell was almost twice their age, and had been a protecting "housemother" to them. When she disappeared after leaving the Bush Company on September 7, 1980, Fulton and Stewart started making inquiries around Fourth Avenue to find her.

Soon after they began their search, the women were told that if they didn't quit asking about Futrell, they "might disappear too." The Mafia wasn't anxious to have the police poking around the Avenue.

The two women knew that Gilbert Pauole had beaten Futrell at least once and had threatened to kill her. Also, Lisa had told them that a bar owner named "Mexican Ray" had threatened her life. Despite the potentially violent repercussions, the two dancers went to the police to report their friend's disappearance. But almost three years after their courageous act, Lisa Futrell was still listed among the missing.

Of course, the women of Fourth Avenue weren't the only ones missing in Anchorage or Alaska. For years the state's justice information system had carried more than 200 names of persons who'd disappeared, about half of them being women. The roster included lost hunters, trappers, boaters and fishermen, bush pilots, prospectors, and runaways. Given the young, transient population in Alaska, particularly since the beginning of the pipeline boom in the seventies, the list was probably an undercount.

Considering the isolated and transient existence of the nude dancers and prostitutes in the tenderloin district, the troopers feared their list of missing was probably an undercount too.

Chapter 6

The day he'd decided to place the singles ad, Hansen began to suggest to his wife that she take a European trip with their twelve-year-old daughter and eight-year-old son as soon as school let out—a long vacation. He wanted the house all to himself for entertaining respondents to his ad—he would call it his "summer project."

Mrs. Hansen quickly warmed to the idea of the trip, seeming more than happy to get away. Before her husband had read the first replies to his ad, she'd planned an itinerary that included a stay in Austria with family friends, then a few weeks in Denmark with Robert's relatives. A friend, Dennise Gold, and her son were going to accompany the Hansens on their trip.

Robert Hansen would later talk about what he'd hoped to find in the thirty or so responses he received. "I wanted to find someone to be close to, a warm relationship, a close friend—noncommercial. I wanted it to be relaxed, not have to be scared the whole time."

In part Hansen's plan may have been a last, pathetic attempt at mid-life to deal with some of the rejection he experienced in adolescence; rejection he'd described to several psychiatrists over the years:

"If you look at my face, from the pockmarks you can tell that I used to have a tremendous amount of acne. I was addicted to sweets, still am.

"When I was a teenager, my face was always one big yellow pimple. Consequently, I never had any girls interested in me. I'd ask a girl out, and she'd say, 'Well no, I'm sorry, I've got something else planned.' I heard that so doggone many times.

"It's hard to explain what it's like to always be wanting, to see others go out on dates. I was just seeing everybody else get theirs."

From the photos and letters he received, Hansen selected respondents he found interesting, and did some preliminary screening while his wife and children were still in town. He met and had coffee with several women; some gave him their phone number and told him to call. One worked at the State Trooper's station, and Hansen stopped by her workplace to meet her. She gave him her number, but she never heard from him. Hansen may have come to the conclusion that he took a chance going to trooper headquarters, and decided not to pursue a potentially risky situation.

A woman who worked at Harry's Restaurant answered Hansen's ad because he owned an airplane. She was interested in flying, taking pilot lessons, so Hansen flew her in his plane to a couple of spots along the Knik River and Lake George. The relationship fizzled.

The first night his family was out of Alaska, Hansen had dinner with a respondent who worked at the International Inn out by the airport. Things went reasonably well, so they went out a few more times—one night it was dancing at the Peanut Farm.

Then, on June 8, the woman celebrated her birthday with Hansen. After dinner at a restaurant, they went to his house and he took her down to his den in the basement to show her his hunting trophies. After he recited his bow-hunting accomplishments, they sat on the couch and watched some TV. Later, Hansen put on a tape and they danced.

The couple settled on the couch again and did a little necking. Then Hansen asked his date if she'd go upstairs and go to bed with him.

"No, I'm not ready for that," she answered.

"Gee whiz, we don't have to go upstairs, we can lay on the floor on the bear rug."

"No," she said, "I don't care to do that either."

Hansen didn't force her.

He maintained he never had sexual relations with any of the women who answered his ad, nor threatened or harmed any of them. "I never met one lady who wasn't just one heck of a nice person, and I enjoyed being with them."

Several of the respondents he dated were eventually interviewed. Besides expressing embarrassment, and relief that they'd escaped unharmed, many indicated their surprise that such a polite and soft-spoken man could have perpetrated so much violence on other women. But behind the courteous manner and folksy "gee whiz, heck" language of Robert Hansen was an urge that had to be satisfied.

To him it seemed there were two kinds of women—the "good," whom he treated with kid gloves of respect, and the "bad," who were *fair game* for whatever he wanted. Whether he really believed the latter or it was his rationalization for his sexual violence, one thing was certain—he had been able to get away with it *for twelve years!*

Five days after the woman turned down his proposition for sex on the bear rug, Robert Hansen was driving west on Fifth Avenue, eating some candy and wearing a prophylactic. *He was hunting.*

Chapter 7

Monday, June 13, 12:00 Midnight

On Sunday night the bars on Fourth and Fifth avenues were quiet. In the midst of single-story, boxlike buildings that formed the "tenderloin strip" in downtown Anchorage, business wasn't as brisk as the midnight air. Nineteen-year-old Cindy Paulson stood on the corner of Fifth and Denali with a lot of territory to herself.

When Cindy felt no one was looking, her hands stayed in her jacket pockets and her demeanor expressed boredom. It had been a slow week, and last night a john had finked out on an appointment. On top of everything else, tonight she was having cramps. It was still daylight, however, and that was at least something that made Anchorage better than the midnight streets of L.A., San Francisco, or Portland.

Cindy spotted a car passing the Mackay Building. When it headed toward her, she postured her five-six frame, cocked her chin, and put a sensual bend into one of her legs. She was "doin' business." As the car approached and slowed down, Cindy recognized the green Buick Century. It was the john who had stood her up last night, so the price would be higher.

Cindy Paulson stepped to the curb, bent down and rested her forearms on the open front passenger window. "Well, Mr. 'Day Late,' you're in luck, I'm here! What's it gonna be?"

Robert Hansen sat at the wheel in jeans, a brown shirt, and green down jacket, wearing a bright green baseball cap. Staring through his glasses, a half smile on his forty-four-year-old, pockmarked face, he replied, "I wanna blowjob."

"It'll be three hundred."

"Too much. One fifty."

"It's gotta be two fifty."

"Look, I have a rubber on."

Cindy's eyes dropped for a moment, then returned to Hansen's face. "Okay, two hundred."

"Sure. Get in."

Paulson opened the door, brushed some candy wrappers off the seat, and got in. "Pull into that parking lot."

Hansen drove into the lot and turned off the engine.

"Put the seat all the way back," Cindy said.

Hansen complied, and she got down to business. What she liked about giving head was that she didn't have to fake anything. It was minimal involvement, and it paid good.

When she thought Hansen was close to coming, Paulson worked faster to get it over with. His breathing became staccato and she could sense his thigh muscles tighten. As she heard his short gasps, she felt his hand begin to play with her neck.

"S-Stop." His upper body moved forward and the fingers of his right hand tightened around a handful of Cindy's brown hair.

Suddenly she was jerked upright and the barrel of a .357 Magnum yawned in her face. From behind the cold, blue barrel she heard a snarling, deliberate voice. "All right, now you'll do exactly what I say. I know what I'm doing . . . I've done this before. So just sit and stay still . . . uh, fasten your seat belt."

In the slow motion of terror, Cindy complied. Her captor reached under the seat, came up with a pair of handcuffs and grinned. "We're going to my house."

Hansen cuffed Cindy and put the gun to her face. He clicked the action. "Now remember, don't move . . . be quiet."

The gun on his lap, he readjusted the seat, started the car, drove out of the lot and turned north. At Third Avenue he made a right and headed east to Sitka Street, where he made another right.

Terrified, Cindy stared straight ahead as they stopped at the intersection at Fifth. She barely noticed the acres of private planes in front of her. Merrill Field was quiet in the nocturnal light.

As they headed east on Fifth, the landing lights of a plane in an approach from the south drew Cindy's glance.

Hansen noticed too. "I'm a pilot, you know."

There was little traffic; Fifth became the Glenn Highway.

"I've taken lots of girls to my house. You do what I say, then everything will be fine."

Hansen made a right at Muldoon Road, and in a few moments the sterility of the suburban strip was left behind as he made another right onto a quiet residential street.

The street's name was Old Harbor. As the car slowed down, Cindy saw a blue-gray ranch nestled in a stand of pines. When Hansen made a right turn into its driveway, she noticed an expansive rack of caribou antlers above the doors of its two-car garage.

"Here we are." Hansen dragged his captive into the house. His grip tightened on her arm as he led her down some steps and into a dark room.

The frightened woman saw brown carpet at her feet when a light went on. Her gaze came up and she was confronted with a menagerie of icy stares. The walls around a couch were covered with stuffed trophy mounts—fish, Dall sheep, mountain goats, a grizzly bear, and game birds. Moose racks, caribou antlers, walrus tusks, and beaver and wolverine skins were arranged around the room. A black bear rug was in front of the couch, and behind it was a tiled area containing a pool table and a Foosball game.

Hansen handcuffed Cindy to a support pillar, then wrapped a chain around her neck, securing the chain to a metal ring on the pillar.

He performed anal and vaginal sex on his victim, then lay down on the couch.

Cindy Paulson, half-naked and hanging chained in humiliation and terror, sheepishly declared, "I have to pee."

Her assailant gave a sigh of annoyance, got off the couch and went into the bathroom. He came out with a yellow towel and threw it at her feet. Then he lay back down on the couch and fell asleep with the .357 Magnum resting on his chest.

While he slept, Cindy urinated into the towel, then remained awake in a cold, aching numbness. After a few hours she heard her tormentor stir.

Hansen got up and unchained her, but left the handcuffs on. He started bragging about his hunting—a world record Dall sheep—and showed his captive a trophy plaque.

It was different than the name he'd used to make an appointment with her for Saturday night. She figured that since he let her know his real name, he'd probably decided to kill her. *She would have to escape if she was going to survive!*

But Robert Hansen wasn't finished with his prey. He forced her down onto the bear rug by the couch and assaulted her vaginally.

Done, he let her go into the bathroom to clean herself, telling her to leave the door open while she did it. Cindy noticed that the bathroom window was sealed shut.

"In the bathroom I saw lots of matches from the Sheraton Hotel," Paulson recalled. "While I was cleaning away the semen with a washcloth, he told me that he'd brought seven other women to his house and that he usually kept them for a week. He said that I was so good that he was going to fly me to a cabin for a few days."

When Cindy came out of the bathroom, Hansen uncuffed her so she could dress. Then putting the cuffs back on, he led her upstairs and out to the Buick. Forcing her onto the floor in the back, he covered her with an army blanket.

Cindy heard the back door close and the driver's door open and shut as Hansen got in. The engine started and the car pulled out of the drive; Paulson sensed they were backtracking the route they'd taken earlier.

Hansen drove down the Glenn Highway, heading for Merrill Field.

Paulson felt the car turn left and continue at a much slower speed. It came to a halt and the engine died. She heard her captor shift in the driver's seat, then his voice overhead.

"I'm gonna load my plane. Stay down and don't move—if you try anything, I'll kill you!"

Cindy felt Hansen get out and heard him go around and get something out of the trunk. When she heard his footsteps trail away, she pushed off the blanket and crawled up to the window to see where he'd gone.

As her eyes adjusted to the light, she could see a sign for Airparts Inc. and, between her and the sign, a row of bush planes. She saw Hansen loading something into a blue and white airplane. *Now was her chance!*

Paulson turned and lunged to the driver's side, threw open the door and stumbled out barefoot into the roadway. She ran north toward Fifth Avenue, not yielding to the stabs of pain in her feet.

"Stop, you bitch! Stop or I'll kill you!" Hansen roared from behind. He started after her.

Cindy never looked back; she ran onto Fifth and turned west.

It was about five A.M. Thirty-six-year-old Robert Yount was driving westbound on Fifth Avenue, on his way to work, and Merrill Field was on his left. Suddenly a woman ran out of the airfield and onto the avenue. Yount slowed down.

Through her panting, Cindy heard a vehicle approaching from behind. She stopped and whirled, holding up her handcuffed wrists. "Help me!" she cried, with all the volume she could manage as the truck passed her.

"What the hell . . . ?" The driver glanced in his rearview mirror for a second look. He pulled over and stopped.

When Hansen reached Fifth Avenue and saw a truck braking near the fleeing Paulson, he turned and ran back to his plane.

Cindy ran and jumped into Yount's truck. "He's going to kill me!" she screamed. "Get me out of here. Hurry!"

Yount looked back on the road, but didn't see anyone. "Sure, it'll be all right . . . you're safe." He pulled back onto Fifth.

"I gotta call my boyfriend!" Cindy blurted. "Could you take the next right and drop me at the Mush Inn on Commercial?"

"You bet." Yount looked at the cuffs. "It's okay now . . . calm down. What happened, anyway?"

Airport security guard Brian Demers was on car patrol at Merrill Field when he spotted the vehicle turn into the northeast entrance and disappear among the airplanes. He decided to check it out. Driving slowly, he looked down each roadway separating the rows of planes.

In the last drive of the northeast corner, Demers spotted a green Buick Century and turned toward it. A man wearing a green coat and bright green baseball cap came running out from behind a blue and white Super Cub. Seeing the guard's approach, the man slowed to a walk, casually got into the car and drove slowly toward Fifth. At the avenue, the car sped away eastbound.

Demers didn't pursue, but went to check on the airplanes in the area where he observed the man. He'd noted the Buick's license number: BJZ–775.

Robert Hansen was racing home to do some house cleaning.

Cindy Paulson ran into the Mush Inn and begged the man at the desk to call the Big Timber Motel and ask for Nathan Franklin's room.

Seeing the woman handcuffed and in distress, the clerk placed the call immediately and handed Cindy the phone.

"Nate!" She broke down. "He . . . he was going to kill me!" she sobbed. "Come right away . . . the Mush Inn . . . on Commercial . . . hurry!"

Meanwhile, as soon as Robert Yount checked into work, he called the APD—the Anchorage Police Department.

Officer Gregg Baker began his ten-hour shift at eleven P.M. on Sunday. His current assignment at APD as a field training officer put him on car patrol with rookie police officer Wayne Vance.

The thirty-six-year-old Baker was in his fifth year on the Anchorage police force. The six-foot native Kansan had earned a degree in biology from Kansas University, then joined the Marines for a tour of duty in Vietnam. He married a girl from Iowa, and after a few years on the police force of Bonner Springs, a Kansas City suburb, he drove up to Alaska in the winter of '77 with his wife Wanda and their son Jade.

After working awhile at Chugach State Park, Baker applied for the position of chief of police in Craig, Alaska, a tiny logging and fishing town six hundred miles southeast of Anchorage. It turned out to be a one-man department, but he took the job. However, with the isolation of the town in winter, followed by an influx of heavy-drinking, hard-living fishermen and loggers which tripled the population in the summer, and considering the school situation for their son, the Bakers moved back to Anchorage. Soon after, their second son, Kaleb, was born.

Baker joined the APD in January 1979. He and his family liked being in Anchorage, and he liked the department and his job.

Over six hours into the shift, Baker and his partner Vance stopped their cruiser on the hill above the city's Alaska Railroad station and got out to stretch. Baker's view took in downtown Anchorage to across the Knik Arm, where the Alaska Range sprawled across the horizon. In the northwest, Mount Susitna—"Sleeping Lady"—pushed up into a clear morning sky.

At 5:29 A.M. the relaxed look on Baker's German-Saxon features dissolved as he and Vance received a radio dispatch:

> ". . . investigate circumstances involving a white female adult picked up by our complainant and taken to the Mush Inn. Female is said to be handcuffed, has medium-brown hair, wearing purple jacket, Levi's, and no shoes. *Code Two* [no lights or siren]."

The officers got into their car and headed for the Mush Inn, wondering if the complaint was for real. "Handcuffed . . . no shoes . . ." Was this one of those crazy calls that sometimes came in early in the morning?

Chapter 8

Robert Hansen had done some thinking as he policed his den and threw the soiled towel and washcloth into the washing machine.

At five-thirty A.M. he telephoned his friend, John Henning.

"Hello?" Henning yawned.

"John, this is Bob. Sorry to bother you so early, but I gotta serious problem. Can you meet me at my shop right away?"

"Well, I guess . . . sure." Henning wondered what the hell could be going on.

In a few minutes he pulled into the small shopping center on the southwest corner of Ninth Avenue and Ingra, a boxlike wooden structure with a tile facade. Robert was waiting outside, under the black-on-white sign: HANSEN'S BAKERY.

"Thanks for coming, John."

"Bob, what's this all about?" Henning asked as he lifted his 240-plus pounds out of the driver's seat.

"John, last night . . . well, my wife and kids are in Europe. I was lonely, so . . . well, I picked up a prostitute and took her to my house. We had sex . . . then she raised the price.

"I wouldn't pay it . . . you know, a deal is a deal, right, John? Anyway, just because I wouldn't pay more, she's hollerin' rape!"

Henning listened quietly. He was a hunting and fishing buddy of Bob's. His friend was upset, stuttering more than usual.

"I can't let this hurt my wife and kids." Hansen explained that he figured he might be arrested, so he'd need an alibi. "Let's get some breakfast—I'll buy. Meet you at Peggy's."

They each drove to Peggy's Café on Fifth Avenue, across from Merrill Field.

At the Mush Inn, Baker and Vance questioned the night clerk, who'd also called the Anchorage police. The clerk described a frightened, barefoot, and handcuffed woman who said she'd been abducted, raped, and was in fear for her life. A man named Franklin, he said, came in a Yellow Cab to pick her up.

Now the officers knew something was going on—but was it a civil or domestic situation, a "trick" gone awry or an actual crime? Baker and Vance drove to the

Big Timber, Baker requesting Dispatch to get a confirmation on the Yellow Cab's destination and to send a backup unit there.

The clerk at the Big Timber Motel said a Nathan Franklin was registered in number 110. Patrolmen Ron Becker and Harry Hanson arrived as backup, and Becker stayed at the desk while the other officers went to Franklin's room. An upset Cindy Paulson, alone and still handcuffed, opened the door for them.

She was hysterical, but calmed down quickly after Baker used a master key to get the cuffs off. With the victim in no apparent danger, Officer Hanson left to get Becker and go back on patrol.

Cindy was what police term a "good victim." She was able to recount events to Baker and Vance, giving specific details about her assailant's appearance, his vehicle, his house—even the street it was on—and she described the den and the wood-handled revolver that had been put to her head.

The bondage and multiple assaults she told about sounded bizarre to the officers, but Baker believed her right away. His instincts told him she was telling the truth.

Paulson gathered a change of clothes, and the police officers took her to their car to transport her to Humana Hospital for a physical exam. They left a message at the motel desk for Nathan Franklin to come down to police headquarters for questioning.

Baker informed Dispatch that a rape had occurred, gave a description of the scene of the assault and the name of the street it was on, and relayed a description of the suspect and his vehicle.

At 5:53 A.M. Dispatch directed officers Hanson and Becker to proceed to Old Harbor Avenue and investigate.

As they passed Merrill Field on the way to the hospital, Cindy told Baker and Vance where Hansen parked his airplane, so they swung into the airstrip to take a look. As they did, a blue and white plane was taking off.

"There, that's his plane!" she shouted.

Quickly, Baker notified Dispatch, who contacted Merrill tower. The pilot was directed to circle back and land.

When they got to where Paulson recalled the plane being parked, there it was, still tied down. The plane taking off was a blue and white lookalike.

Meanwhile, Security Guard Brian Demers saw the police car and came over to see what was going on. He told the two officers what he'd witnessed forty-five minutes earlier in the vicinity of the Super Cub they were examining, and gave them the plate number of the green Buick Century he'd seen parked by the plane until it sped away.

Resuming the trip to Humana, Baker gave Dispatch the Buick's license number to trace and asked for a registration check on a blue and white Super Cub, tail number N3089Z. He asked that Merrill tower be requested to detain that plane if it tried to take off.

Gregg Baker saw everything falling into place, verifying what Cindy had told them. He began to consider that this could be something more than a rape, and wondered if it could be connected to the missing dancer cases. If so, how they approached the suspect could be important.

Baker advised Dispatch that it was a "critical situation"; the suspect had a gun, but if spotted, he should only be detained, not arrested.

At 6:22 A.M., APD Dispatch called Merrill tower to find out the registered owner of the Super Cub. The tower said it couldn't do an "R/O" on an airplane, but provided the telephone number of the Federal Aeronautics Administration, which could. The tower promised to detain a takeoff by the plane in question.

The FAA gave APD the registered owner of the Super Cub: "Robert C. Hansen, 7223 Old Harbor Avenue, Anchorage," and agreed to inform the police if Hansen tried to file a flight plan.

As Vance turned the squad car into the Humana Hospital parking lot, Dispatch radioed Baker that the registrations of the Buick and plane matched.

More of Cindy Paulson's story had been confirmed.

Chapter 9

At Peggy's Café the aroma of baking pies mingled with the smells of coffee, flapjacks, and bacon and eggs.

Over breakfast, Robert Hansen and John Henning formulated the alibi they'd give if it became necessary: Bob had come to Henning's apartment around twelve-thirty that morning, and they'd been together until after five.

Henning considered he "was helping a friend in need."

Robert paid the tab and they went outside.

"John, one more thing." Hansen took a gun case out of his car that contained the .357 Magnum and his .223 Mini-Ruger 14. "I'd appreciate you taking these for safekeeping for me."

Henning's brows dipped. It seemed to him an odd request, but he shrugged off his wariness. "Sure thing."

"Well, I'm going home now, John. I suppose the police will be there."

Officers Becker and Hanson arrived at Old Harbor Avenue and checked out all the houses on the street. They observed caribou antlers above the garage at 7223, and as the registration information on the suspect's vehicle and plane trickled in from Dispatch, it was clear that it was the address where the assault occurred.

There appeared to be no one at home, and there was no sign of the green Buick. Two other vehicles in the driveway checked out as registered to Hansen.

Becker and Hanson went to opposite ends of Old Harbor Avenue and waited.

At Humana Hospital, Officer Baker asked the doctor in charge to be watchful for any signs of redness caused by restraints on Cindy Paulson's neck and arms, and for any abrasions around her abdomen and vaginal area. The officers stayed in the waiting room while Cindy was taken away to be examined.

A victim of rape usually has the immediate urge to wash away the assault with a shower and a change of clothing, with the clothes worn during the attack being thrown away or directly into a washer. The handcuffs had inhibited Paulson from following through on that urge, so the exam held greater promise of providing substantial forensic evidence.

The examination is an ordeal rape victims must endure if they're going to press charges for the assault. There's a standard procedure for an evidentiary exam of a female victim, and each step and specimen taken is carefully documented and logged. Subsequent transfer or transport of any physical evidence from the exam is also carefully documented to preserve what's called "the chain of evidence."

To begin, the victim's clothing is removed and examined for rips, missing buttons, and stains. An ultraviolet Woods light is passed over any stains to test for the presence of acid phosphatose from seminal fluid—a fluorescent-blue glow indicates a positive test. Then the clothing is folded and placed in a brown paper bag and labeled. A paper bag is used to allow air to circulate and preserve any evidence; nonmotile sperm, for example, can last up to twelve months in fabric.

The victim receives a general physical: temperature, pulse, blood pressure. Then a speculum is inserted into her vagina, and vaginal fluids are aspirated and contained for testing. The speculum is removed, and the doctor proceeds with a gynecological exam, checking the vagina and rectum for injuries.

Any particles or loose hairs on the victim's body are collected for testing. The victim is asked to supply urine and saliva samples, and fingernail scrapings are collected. Finally, the Woods light is passed over the victim's body to detect any acid phosphatose activity from seminal fluid residue.

Cindy Paulson's exam yielded immediate evidence of vaginal penetration and ejaculation—a tampon found in her vagina was fluorescent under the Woods light, saturated with seminal fluid.

Meanwhile, in the waiting room, Baker was called to the phone and informed that his sergeant, Mack Strutko, was coming to Humana to assist, and that the officers investigating on Old Harbor Avenue had reported that the victim's description of the house's exterior matched perfectly. Baker was about to hang up when he was told that Officer Becker had just alerted Dispatch that the suspect's vehicle was approaching the residence, so he stayed on the line.

At 6:51 A.M., Robert Hansen arrived at his house.

Becker and Officer Hanson converged—Becker in the squad car to block the drive. He received an update of the suspect's description from Dispatch: ". . . pockmarked face and neck, fifty years old, scruffy graying hair, uneven front teeth, with brown shirt, bright green cap, and jeans. Suspect is said to stutter."

"Robert Hansen?"

"Yes. What can I do for you, officers?"

Immediately Becker reported to Dispatch, "We have all of that here except the gray hair."

When Baker received the news of the make on Hansen, he got off the phone and instructed Vance to stand by at the hospital to look after Cindy. Then he ran out to the parking lot to meet Sergeant Strutko.

As they headed for Old Harbor Avenue, Baker briefed Strutko on what he knew so far. The sergeant saw how things were fitting together, and began talking about how the situation should be handled.

At this point Anchorage police procedures had to take into account a Supreme Court decision that a person cannot be arrested at their own home on probable-cause evidence. The only exception is an arrest done "in hot pursuit," which will even then probably be challenged in court. If the challenge is successful, any evidence obtained under the circumstances without a warrant or consent to search, no matter how conclusive, can and probably will be thrown out of court.

Strutko told Dispatch to direct that Hansen's residence and vehicle be secured until he and Baker could get there.

Back on Old Harbor Avenue, Robert Hansen agreed to a request that he voluntarily go to police headquarters for questioning. Becker drove the suspect downtown, and the other officer stayed at the scene.

In a few minutes Strutko and Baker pulled up at 7223 Old Harbor.

"Sarge, look at that rack of caribou antlers on the garage . . . it's just like she described."

Strutko ordered Officer Hanson to remain and keep the house and Buick secure, and then said to Baker, "I'll take you back to Humana to pick up the victim. Next, we'll go downtown and have Investigations get some warrants."

At the hospital the examining doctor informed the officers about the seminal fluid in the tampon, but reported that the only abrasions he'd observed had been around Cindy Paulson's wrists. Baker signed for the exam report and physical evidence, which included the clothes and hair samples, then put them into an evidence bag with the handcuffs he'd removed from Cindy's wrists. The tampon, blood samples, swabs, and semen samples would remain at the hospital under refrigeration.

Vance and Baker escorted Paulson to their car and headed downtown.

Chapter 10

As Patrolman Becker approached APD headquarters, he received a radio message from Lieutenant Doug Jones: "Take the suspect to Investigations."

William Dennis, of APD's Sexual Assault Unit, had come in early to take charge of the alleged rape case. He reviewed the dispatch reports and was briefed by Becker when he brought the suspect in. At 7:45 A.M., Investigator Dennis sat down across from Robert Hansen to begin the interrogation. For some reason, Dennis couldn't figure why, the suspect looked familiar.

The man with the pockmarked face came on with what police term a "soft denial," politely disavowing any knowledge of the kidnap and rape or having seen or been with a prostitute the night before. Soft denials usually make police suspicious, particularly in rape cases, where innocent suspects generally feel outraged and become indignant when accused.

Hansen told Dennis that he'd spent the first part of the evening at the house of his longtime friend, John Sumrall, where they worked until about eleven-thirty P.M. putting a hinge on a seat for Hansen's airplane. He said he left Sumrall's and went directly to the home of another friend, John Henning, and they sat up until five-thirty A.M. drinking beer and planning a fishing trip. Then the two of them went to Merrill Field and installed the airplane seat in his Super Cub.

When Hansen gave him the phone numbers of the two friends, Dennis went to find a phone.

Arriving at APD, Baker and Vance took Paulson to an interview room and left her with a representative from a rape crisis center and a police officer who would take Cindy's statement.

After checking the evidence bag into locker 46 and getting Vance started on the paperwork, Baker headed to Investigations, where William Dennis was checking out Hansen's alibi. Sumrall and Henning verified their friend's story.

Meanwhile, once again Cindy Paulson was giving a detailed description of her rape, her assailant, and his car, house, and plane. The interview completed, the officer went to Investigations to give Dennis and Baker its summary. Lieutenant Jones and Sergeant Mack Strutko joined the conference.

Gregg Baker described what happened:

Cindy was being consistent, sticking to her story. But a strong disagreement developed; in fact, things got pretty heated. Strutko and I were convinced that Cindy was telling the truth. We'd seen plenty of evidence corroborating her story, and we were primed to go after it.

Dennis and the lieutenant thought Cindy was lying . . . they did concede that Hansen could be lying too. They suspected a "trick gone awry"—an argument between a hooker and her john. The two of them just stuck to that assumption.

Strutko and I pushed. We wanted warrants.

Finally Lieutenant Jones called the District Attorney's office to get a third opinion. The first thing the D.A. asked was whether or not Hansen had said no to consent searches.

"Ah, well, he hasn't been asked," Jones replied, realizing that Hansen should have been, as part of standard procedures.

"So do it!" barked the voice in the receiver.

Hansen, continuing to be polite and cooperative, signed search waivers for his house, Buick, and airplane. He accompanied Dennis and Baker to 7223 Old Harbor, talking very little on the way—just a few words about hunting.

They searched the Buick first, and William Dennis's report concluded, "Nothing of evidentiary value found." Baker, however, took into account Cindy Paulson's description of her assailant's attire and noted "a green down jacket in the front seat and a bright green baseball cap in the rear window." Also, Baker's report mentioned two trash bags of candy wrappers in the car, some rolled up Ace bandages on the dashboard, and a box of .223 cartridges underneath the front seat.

Hansen and the officers entered the house and went directly to the den. Dennis and Baker observed all the hunting trophies Cindy had described, and saw the large bear hide on the carpet in front of the couch. A Foosball game and a pool table were in a tiled area, just like she said.

Dennis studied the center support beam, saw one hole, but found "no threadmarks going in or out of the support." In the bathroom Baker found "several matchbooks from the Sheraton Hotel."

Neither officer found the towel or washcloth Cindy described, and both indicated in their reports that they found no evidence of bondage in the den. However, on the south side of the basement they did find a false panel that Dennis reported "was observed to carry [behind it] a large number of guns, both handguns and rifles and shotguns." There wasn't the wood-handled revolver Cindy had described, but the handguns in the weapons cache would become significant.

The men went upstairs and continued to search for the chain, washcloth, and the towel Cindy Paulson said she had urinated in. After checking the living portion of the upstairs and finding nothing, they moved on to the garage, where they found ammunition, shell-reloading equipment, animal traps, machines, and tools. Baker noted "a stack of army blankets, the type the victim said she was covered with while being taken to the airport."

After searching the house, the officers stepped outside with their suspect.

"Now, we'll go to Merrill and have a look at your airplane," said Dennis, giving Hansen the keys to the Buick. "You lead the way."

As the men left Old Harbor Avenue, Nathan Franklin was downtown at Anchorage police headquarters making a statement. He said he was called to the Mush Inn around five o'clock that morning by Cindy Paulson, and that when he picked her up, she was handcuffed, upset, and had no shoes. When he took her back to their room at the Big Timber Motel, she had told him about a guy who had raped her and threatened to kill her.

At Merrill Field, Hansen couldn't find the keys to his Super Cub; he thought they were in his car. A spare set he had taped to the fuselage had come loose and fallen down into the belly of the plane, and Hansen couldn't reach them.

"Let me give it a shot." Investigator Dennis stretched, strained, and retrieved the keys, but the search yielded no evidence.

Shortly after ten A.M. Dennis thanked Hansen for his cooperation and told him he could go.

Robert Hansen left Merrill and headed to his bakery, mulling over the morning's close call and wondering what he should do next. He decided he'd call John Henning when he got to the bakery.

At noon, over beer and pizza, Hansen and Henning talked about lining up a third party to corroborate the alibi. Henning had a friend, a taxi driver, who owed him a favor.

"Bob, when we finish here we'll go see the guy. By the way, do you have an attorney?"

"No, but I do have a legal fund with the Teamsters."

"It'd probably be a good idea to talk to a lawyer."

"Yeah. John, can you think how I might get the girl's address? Maybe, if I paid her the extra money, she'd forget the whole thing."

Henning had no idea what his friend's real intentions might be.

"Gee, Bob, I don't know . . . say, they probably took her to Humana. That's the one police and fire use for everything. I know a doctor there . . . I'll give him a call and see what I can find out."

The two men finished their lunch, then went to find Henning's friend. The taxi driver agreed to back up Hansen's alibi.

Returning home, Hansen called the Teamsters Legal Services and lined up an attorney. Later that evening he got a call from Henning.

"Bob, no luck with that doctor. He said they just don't release that kind of information . . . privacy and all that."

That policy probably saved Cindy Paulson's life.

Chapter 11

During the course of a rape investigation, as a kind of tactic for emotional survival, victims sometimes begin to minimize what happened during the assault. Cindy Paulson's story changed the day after the assault, when she was reinterviewed by Investigator William Dennis at police headquarters:

Asked how many times Robert Hansen had assaulted her, she said, "Just once . . . vaginal, on the bearskin rug."

Perhaps the officer's attitude prompted her to change her story to lessen her feelings of humiliation.

Viewing a photo lineup, Cindy immediately picked out Hansen's picture as her assailant.

When Paulson left, Dennis telephoned John Henning, who again affirmed that from Sunday midnight until about five-thirty Monday morning he'd been with Robert Hansen and another friend.

"That's the way it was. I'm not lying about it."

On his way home Monday, Gregg Baker had searched Dumpsters between Merrill Field and Hansen's home in Muldoon, hoping that he might find something Hansen discarded in haste—the towel, chain, or Cindy Paulson's shoes. He'd found nothing.

During his patrol on Tuesday, he returned to Merrill Field and talked with security guard Brian Demers, whose account remained consistent with the story he told the day before. At the end of his shift, Baker got Robert Yount's work number from Dispatch; he wanted to interview the original complainant.

Yount told him about picking up a barefoot woman by Merrill Field, who was handcuffed and hysterical, and screaming that someone raped her and was going to kill her. He didn't, however, see anyone chasing her.

After talking with Yount, Baker decided to back off. It was Investigations' case; he might be stepping on some toes if he continued to poke around.

Wednesday, Investigator William Dennis discussed the Paulson case with Assistant D.A. Steven Branchflower. Robert Hansen had a criminal history in Alaska, beginning with a conviction for assault with a deadly weapon in 1971. Coincidentally, Branchflower had assisted in prosecuting a felony-theft conviction of Hansen in 1977. However, having been involved in hundreds of other cases since that time, the assistant prosecutor didn't remember the case or Robert Hansen.

Most police officials agree that a District Attorney gets a feel for a case through the way it's presented to him or her by the cop. If the cop is shaky about the case, the D.A. picks up on that and develops the same perspective. After reviewing the Paulson case with Dennis, Branchflower concluded that he wouldn't seek any warrants at that time, because "there was no corroborating evidence that the victim had ever been inside Hansen's house."

Friday, June 17th, Dennis asked Cindy Paulson to come down to police headquarters for a lie detector test. The next day, she and Nathan Franklin left Anchorage without her taking the test or notifying police of their departure.

The following Monday, Investigator Dennis had a visitor at APD—Fred Dewey, Robert Hansen's attorney. They discussed the Paulson case for two and a half hours.

Dennis explained the charges under investigation were rape and kidnapping, but he couldn't say whether Dewey's client would be arrested or not. He allowed the attorney to read through the police reports and files compiled in the case.

Significant was an affidavit Dewey later filed in Superior Court, wherein he stated that the materials he reviewed at that meeting contained reports of Hansen's criminal record in Alaska, which included arrests for kidnap and rape, and convictions for assault with a deadly weapon and felony theft. In addition, Hansen's record mentioned a conviction for arson in Iowa in 1961.

Aside from the glaring kidnap-rape charges, the three felony convictions in Hansen's records had important implications, considering what Dennis had observed during his search of Hansen's house. In his report of the June 13 search, the investigator wrote that he saw "handguns" in the hidden weapons cache. A convicted felon is forbidden by law to possess a handgun, and each sidearm represents a separate violation of the law—a felony.

Assuming "handguns" to mean at least "two," Hansen would be answerable to a minimum of two felony charges, with a possible five-year sentence on each count. Dennis overlooked this.

Another document that Dewey filed in Superior Court questioned the procedures of Dennis's investigation. It pointed out that police officers failed to do a trace metal test on Hansen's hands—trace metal can be found on a person's hand if they've held a weapon or metal object in the last twenty-four to forty-eight hours. Further, the affidavit stated that during the search of Hansen's house on June 13, no fingerprint dusting or preservation was done, and police officers failed to vacuum the house to preserve fibers and hair samples that could have been on the premises.

The trace metal test was not a standard investigative procedure at APD in 1983; in fact, it wasn't being used by any law enforcement agency in Alaska. But the omission of the forensic work and preservation was another matter.

In a sworn affidavit Dennis admitted that during his investigation and search of Hansen's property, no evidence was seized, even though there were items found that corroborated Cindy Paulson's story. Also, he acknowledged that no photographs were taken of the suspect's house, car, or airplane, nor was there any forensic work done.

The officer went on to defend his investigation, stating that at the time of the search he had no knowledge of the suspect's criminal record, but that he did know Mr. Hansen had a family and was a "man of means" who owned a bakery, house, airplane, and several vehicles. On the other hand, the investigator said, he'd been told that the complainant worked as a prostitute.

Dennis concluded his statement:

> I consider myself to be a courteous person. Having been raised in the South, I was taught to be that way. . . . As a matter of courtesy to a seemingly upright, well-to-do businessman, I searched only in a limited way to find certain items, and when these did not turn up, I stopped the search.

Society tends to judge "who" or "what" a man is by what he has. Officer Dennis fell into that trap. That, coupled with his bias against a "woman of the streets," undermined his investigation to the point that he ignored facts and corroborating evidence in the case.

Six days after she left Anchorage, on June 24, Cindy Paulson was in Portland at the corner of Yamhill Street and Southwest Ninth Avenue, and was arrested by police and booked for soliciting for prostitution.

At 9:55 A.M. the following Monday, Investigator Dennis drove to the Big Timber Motel to talk to Cindy Paulson. The manager told him that she and Nathan Franklin had left on June 18, probably headed for Oregon. They'd left unpaid a large phone bill to a number which, Dennis found out, belonged to the Sixth Avenue Motel in downtown Portland. No Cindy Paulson or Nathan Franklin was registered there.

Dennis called the Portland Police Department and was routed to a Detective Trummer in the Drug and Vice Division. He asked Trummer to do a records check on Cindy R. Paulson and get back to him.

Two hours later Trummer called. His department's files had her as Felisha Lee Redmond. She'd been arrested for prostitution just three days before. The detective told Dennis he would send him the information and a photograph of Redmond to confirm the alias.

When the color photo arrived, Dennis compared it to the one of the victim on file. Cindy Paulson and Felisha Redmond were one and the same. Their birth years were the same, but Redmond's birthday was July 5 and Cindy's was January 7.

The officer studied Redmond's rap sheet. The computer printout listed arrests in San Francisco, Los Angeles, and Portland, all for prostitution.

Summarizing these findings in his report, Dennis wrote that Cindy Paulson was "apparently in good health," and concluded:

DISPOSITION: This case is CLOSED EXCEPTIONAL CLEARANCE. No further action by INV. DENNIS.

Chapter 12

The petite blonde got out of her car and swung the door closed. After taking a few steps, she turned around, went back to the vehicle, and stooped to look in the side mirror—there was just a hint of redness in her eyes now. Judy Vigoren had been crying during most of the drive to the trooper station on Tudor Road; she cried a lot when she was alone. Judy took a deep breath and resumed her walk to the station entrance.

The woman at the security desk put a clip-on visitor badge by the pen next to the open logbook. "Would you sign in please, Mrs. Vigoren? I'll let Sergeant Haugsven know you're here."

The procedure was the same as when she'd come to see Sergeant Haugsven in February, and the situation hadn't changed since then—Judy Vigoren's daughter, Tami Pederson, had been missing since August 1982. The anguish was tearing at Judy's heart and putting a severe strain on her marriage.

During the past ten months, memories of her daughter crowded Judy Vigoren's thoughts and dreams. Remembering her daughter's birth could bring both a smile and tears to her face; Tami Joy had been an eight-pound, thirteen-ounce baby with big, sparkling blue eyes.

Tami's birth weight only doubled in her first year, however, and she'd grown up to be a petite five-foot-two with dark blond hair like her mother's.

"Joy" proved to be an appropriate middle name for Tami; her zest for life was irrepressible. She was popular and did well in school, interested in creative writing and journalism. Good in gymnastics, she also excelled in dance and ballet. Tami Pederson's mother and stepfather were proud of their daughter.

And Tami was a caring sister, being very protective of her younger half brother, Tony. He continued to be her "little brother" even after he reached six-foot-three and 200 pounds.

Judy's first husband was Tami's natural father, but Vern Pederson had adopted her shortly after he and Judy were married, when Tami was eighteen months old. Vern's and Judy's marriage fell on troubled times in the late seventies, and divorce proceedings began.

At that point there was a change in their daughter's behavior. She began having trouble in school and wanted to drop out. The day Vern and Judy's divorce became final, Tami wrote an expletive on the blackboard at school and walked out—she didn't finish her junior year. She never returned to high school, but did earn an equivalency degree and later enrolled in writing courses at a Seattle junior college.

A typical teenager, Tami Pederson liked clothes and went along with the trends. She waitressed and got good tips, and the money went toward her social life and wardrobe.

She began to run with a fast crowd. Shortly after her nineteenth birthday, in November 1981, she go-go-danced on amateur night at a nightspot operated by the Colacurcio family in the Seattle suburb of Woodinville. She won first prize, and the $75 cash prize was enough for Tami to buy a rabbit jacket she wanted.

After the contest, a man from the Talents West booking agency approached her with an offer of a dancing job in Alaska. He promised her airfare to Anchorage, housing there, and the opportunity to earn several hundred dollars a day.

To make lots of money sounded great to Tami. She had thought of going to Las Vegas to audition for the shows there, but this was an actual job offer to dance for good pay. She accepted it.

Tami Pederson got on the plane at the Sea-Tac Airport with a one-way ticket and great expectations, but landed in a lifestyle very different from what she'd imagined. Gilbert Pauole picked her up at the Anchorage International Airport and drove her downtown in his Mercedes to a dingy hotel on Fourth Avenue. Pauole told her she'd be dancing at the Wild Cherry, and that she'd be driven to and from work every day. Tami quickly got the impression that her boss wanted to control her every move.

The Wild Cherry was a drab, wooden, and windowless boxlike structure, and its interior didn't begin to approach that of any swank Vegas club or lounge. The leering audience coaxed the dancers to take everything off during their routines, and it booed when it didn't get its way. Tami had thought it would be like the go-go dancing she'd done in Woodinville, not nude dancing.

It took her just a couple of days to decide that the job wasn't for her, but when she went to Pauole for a ticket home, he refused. He said she owed *him* money for airfare to Anchorage, rent, and the cost of a dancing costume. When she protested that she'd been promised those expenses would be covered by Talents West, Gilbert Pauole snarled, "That ain't the way it is!"

A scared Tami Pederson called her mother, who wired her some money to get out of Anchorage.

Unfortunately, she wasn't able to find a niche for herself in Seattle, and nine months later Tami took another booking through Talents West and went to Anchorage to dance at the Good Times Lounge. This time Pauole housed her at the Sleeping Lady, an apartment complex he managed as a dormitory for Talents West dancers. Junior Pauole lived on the premises and hovered like a jailer. Using his set of keys, he'd frequently enter the women's apartments unannounced.

Though once again Pederson felt Gilbert Pauole was trying to control her every move, she ignored that and focused on her dancing. Determined to be one of, if not the best, dancers in Anchorage, she created and choreographed her own routines and designed her own costumes, making her dancing—at least to herself—an art form. She seemed to be in relatively good spirits when she flew to Seattle at the end of 1981 to celebrate Christmas with her family, then returned to Anchorage after New Year's.

In March of '82 Tami moved in with her boyfriend, a young man who'd grown up in North Seattle and come up to Alaska to seek his fortune. Past the scowling stare of Gilbert Pauole, the young couple carried Tami's belongings out of the Sleeping Lady. Being in love and out from under the thumb of Pauole, she began to consider Anchorage her home.

The last time Judy saw her daughter was over the following Fourth of July holiday, when she and her third husband, Gary Vigoren, flew up for a family gathering at her sister's home in Soldotna, seventy-five miles southwest of Anchorage on the Kenai Peninsula. Judy thought her daughter seemed happy and very much in love.

In her blue suitcase, Tami had brought along some of her performance costumes, and she danced for the family. No one was comfortable with the fact that Tami was working in a club in Anchorage's tenderloin district, but that didn't change the fact she was a person they loved and cared about very much.

The visit ended at the Soldotna airport, with "little brother" Tony and mother Judy giving Tami good-bye hugs and kisses. They both watched the little plane lift off the runway and head toward Anchorage.

Back in Seattle a few days later, Judy Vigoren had a phone conversation with her daughter, who told her that she'd had a fight with her boyfriend and was staying with some friends at the Sleeping Lady. They talked again on August 7, and Tami said she thought she and her boyfriend were going to get back together soon.

Judy tried to call Tami the following week, but found the phone had been disconnected. When she finally got hold of someone in Gilbert Pauole's office in the Wild Cherry, no one knew anything about her daughter's whereabouts.

Anxiety snowballed as several months went by without any word from or about her daughter. Periodic checks with her ex-husband Vern Pederson yielded the same depressing news: he hadn't heard from her either.

The Vigorens had a construction business, so they decided to look into bidding some jobs in Alaska—they could combine business with looking for Tami. In February of '83 they flew up to Anchorage, and Vern Pederson went with them.

While Judy and Gary investigated business prospects and collected bid specifications, Vern went around to the topless clubs and bars, trying to find some information about his daughter's whereabouts.

Judy Vigoren recalled the search was very hard on her ex-husband: "It really bothered Vern going to those places on Fourth Avenue. He didn't like what he saw. He always loved Tami very much . . . he couldn't have loved her more than if she were his own."

Going to the State Trooper station to report Tami missing, Judy met with Sergeant Lyle Haugsven. Her heart sank when she found out other women were missing from downtown Anchorage; suddenly, hope for her daughter's safe return was being squashed by a fear that she'd never see her again. Upset, she requested that Tami be put on the national missing persons list.

Haugsven told her the name would go into the Alaska Justice Information System which was linked to an interstate roster of missing persons.

The Vigorens found promising bid prospects in Anchorage, but they and Vern came up empty-handed on information about Tami.

Back in Seattle, the Vigorens prepared bids for the Anchorage projects, and Judy continued to go to a support group for persons with missing loved ones. There she learned a grim statistic—over ninety percent of marriages where there is a missing child end up in divorce because of the resultant stress.

Successful with several bids, the Vigorens set up shop in Anchorage that summer. Judy was the secretary and bookkeeper for the business, and she sold real estate on the side. She wanted to keep as busy as possible; any idle time made her vulnerable to grieving over her missing daughter.

Now, as Tami's mother met with Sergeant Haugsven again, she found him to be the kind and considerate person he'd been before.

Lyle Haugsven sensed the turmoil and desperation behind the woman's controlled demeanor, and he knew from experience that any assurances he might try to give would have little effect. Families and friends of missing persons seek a closure—if not a happy one, at least the relief of a normal grieving at the loss of a loved one. The person sitting across from him wanted answers, but he had none to give.

Chapter 13

Anchorage becomes a center for tourism in the summer. "Outsiders" land at its international airport and fan out into Alaska's expansive wilderness to hike, climb mountains, hunt, fish, and photograph abundant wildlife and awesome scenery.

The Alaska Railroad pulls coaches full of tourists up to Denali Park to see Mount McKinley, and farther north to visit Fairbanks. It runs trains south to Seward, where tourists can see whales, seals, and other marine life in Resurrection Bay.

Bush pilots and guides take the more adventurous visitors to remote areas of pristine grandeur in a territory once nicknamed "Seward's Folly." Boat excursions provide close-up views of glaciers, and buses head north out of Anchorage taking sightseers across the Knik River and into the Mantanuska Valley, where the abundant summer daylight helps produce vegetables of gargantuan size—like eighty-pound cabbages. Other buses go south to Portage Glacier, then onto the Kenai Peninsula, where inland and coastal waters teem with trophy salmon and 200-pound halibut.

While tourists and residents bustled about to enjoy the Alaska summer of '83, troopers investigating the missing dancers case delved through a dark, sordid world of suspects. Though there were several men under suspicion, solid leads were hard to come by.

A promising tip about a porno photographer who all of a sudden had moved to Hawaii was checked out—in some of the dancer disappearances it had been reported that the women vanished when they'd gone to keep an appointment for a photo session. But the lead turned out to be a dead end, so it was back to rehashing the facts.

Though it seemed probable that the murdered and missing were the victims of sex-related violence, at this point the troopers hadn't interviewed a victim who'd escaped or avoided abduction who could confirm it. Was there a calculating kidnapper-rapist-killer stalking vulnerable victims, or a "Jack the Ripper" carrying out a crusade against the "evil women" of Fourth Avenue? The main link between the murdered and missing women continued to be the tenderloin district.

Sergeant Lyle Haugsven and State Trooper Wayne Von Clasen spent a lot of time in the streets and clubs of downtown Anchorage. A unique situation had gradually developed: the women of Fourth Avenue no longer saw the police as adversaries; the dancers knew why the State Troopers were around, and they appreciated it.

"It was like we became one of the family," Von Clasen recalled.

Besides looking for leads in the case and instructing the women on how best to protect themselves, the troopers would walk the dancers to their cars if there was no bouncer or doorman to escort them at the end of their shift. The officers gave out their home phone numbers so they could be reached during off-duty hours, telling the women to call if they felt threatened or saw something suspicious.

It took the troopers a while to get used to the fact that the dancers in the clubs were naked most of the time—not the typical police interview situation. But the women seemed to think nothing of it. Because of their business, their bodies were apart from their person. As Von Clasen put it, "It probably had to be that way for them to cope with it all."

Lyle Haugsven remembered one incident, perhaps the only one during his many months on the case that provided him with the relief of a good laugh.

He was at the Bush Company interviewing a dancer whom he had questioned the day before. Today she sat in the booth with a brief two-piece costume on; the day before, she'd been completely nude during the interview.

As Haugsven and the dancer talked, Bush Company owner Edna Cox ambled over to the booth and said to the dancer, "Don't you think you should put some clothes on while you talk to the sergeant?"

Lyle recalled, "Well, the lady and I looked across the table at each other, both of us thought about how she was *dressed* the day before, and the two of us busted out laughing. Edna shrugged and walked away."

Over the months, the troopers got to know many of the dancers as people; in the atmosphere of trust, the women revealed some of their person. Some had come from pretty rough backgrounds; life hadn't been easy for many of them. Mostly, they were young women trying to survive in the only way they thought they could.

From police, court, parole, and rape crisis center files going back to 1980, the troopers had compiled a list of over thirty suspects. Modern police procedures hold to a tenet from the fourteenth century called "Occam's razor," which can be stated: "If something can be done with fewer assumptions, it's a big waste of time to do it with more." That list of suspects had to be narrowed.

The missing dancers case was at a point so many investigations reach—it needed a break. The troopers didn't want it to come from more disappearances or dead bodies.

Chapter 14

July 29

Anchorage police officer Gregg Baker contemplated the disposition in Investigator William Dennis's final report on the Cindy Paulson case.

"Exceptional Clearance" can mean one of two things: either the complainant asks for a case to be dropped, or runs out of the energy to see it through and lets it die on the vine. Baker suspected that Cindy had been scared off by the lie detector test—the police were normally her adversary; she probably figured the test was something to get her into trouble.

Baker pulled all the reports he could find on Robert Hansen's contact with Anchorage police. Then he found it—twelve years ago, 1971, two arrests for kidnap-rape and assault with a deadly weapon! A pattern consistent with Cindy Paulson's story! And an unusual twist—Officer William Dennis had been in on the first collar in '71!

Now Baker was in a difficult position. He was convinced that the Paulson case should be pursued, and he had a strong hunch it could be related to all the women disappearing on Fourth Avenue. But APD Investigations had dropped the case, and Baker didn't want to jeopardize his relationship with them—after all, that was where he wanted to work eventually. He did know the State Troopers were investigating the missing dancers.

A couple of days later, Baker called Alaska State Trooper Sergeant Jim Stogsdill—the two men had become friends when Baker was police chief down in Craig and Stogsdill was assigned to the trooper station in Sitka.

"Gregg, Sergeant Lyle Haugsven is the man who handles most of the investigation of the dancers," the trooper told his friend. "But listen, if you do send the case over here—no matter how much discretion you use, there's no way it won't eventually get back to APD that you did it."

The next day, Baker talked to APD sergeant Mack Strutko. He laid out the Paulson case situation, saying that he felt he couldn't let its investigation just die.

Strutko mulled it over for a few moments, then looked his officer in the eye. "Gregg, you do what you think is right."

Baker compiled copies of the Paulson case file, Hansen's arrest and conviction records, wrote a cover report, put all the materials in an envelope, and dropped the packet off at AST headquarters on Tudor Road.

Chapter 15

On his way home from the trooper station, Lyle Haugsven stopped at the Safeway in Eagle River and filled up a shopping cart with some "survival food-stuffs." He was looking forward to a few weeks of fishing and hunting—one of the major reasons he liked living in Alaska. His expectations made his wait at the checkout a little more tolerable.

From a line two registers away, an attractive blond woman noticed Haugsven. Bobbie Morehead recognized the sergeant, and when his glance met hers, she raised a hand slightly and gave a half-smile "hello." Then she looked away and moved her cart forward.

When Lyle had returned her greeting, he saw a sadness in her face and sensed her disappointment; he knew she was hoping he'd indicate to her that they should talk a moment, that he had some news about her sister, Sue Luna.

The sergeant wished he did.

Sue Luna had come up to Anchorage in May 1982. She'd grown up in Seattle, married at seventeen, and with her husband in prison for assault and battery, she was struggling alone to raise their four-year-old daughter, Liz. When Sue's mother-in-law offered to take Elizabeth on a long vacation with her, Sue took the opportunity to fly to Anchorage for a six-week dancing stint, the booking arranged by Talents West. She was looking forward to the money she was promised and the chance to visit with her older sister, Bobbie, who ran a restaurant with her husband in Chugiak, fifteen miles north of Anchorage.

Bobbie Morehead didn't know her sister was in Alaska until Sue called her three days after she'd arrived in Anchorage. Sue was a little sheepish about telling her sister that she was dancing at the Good Times Lounge—she knew Bobbie wouldn't be pleased about that.

But Bobbie was delighted that her sister was in Alaska, and asked her when she'd have her first day off. When Sue answered "Tomorrow," Bobbie told her she'd drive down to Anchorage and pick her up.

Sue was more like a daughter than a sister to Morehead—when Bobbie was a teenager, Sue was her "little girl." She took her to all the Disney movies, to the park, all the fun things. "Susie" had been afraid of the dark, and if her little sister came into her room at night, sucking her thumb and dragging her blanket, Bobbie would let Susie crawl in with her.

Bobbie found out her sister had been dancing in Seattle for quite a while, but was planning just a short stay in Anchorage.

Bobbie had read about the missing dancers and warned her sister about the danger. She pointed out to Sue that down in Seattle she'd had the protection of their two brothers, who played in the band where she was dancing. "Up here, you're in that club on your own."

She wanted to give Sue a small, .25-caliber handgun to keep in her purse for protection, but her sister declined, saying that she was scared to death of guns. "I couldn't even bring myself to touch that thing," she told her older sister.

Talents West housed Sue Luna at the Sleeping Lady, along with her friend Robin, who'd come up from Seattle with her. Sue danced at the Good Times Lounge on Dimond Boulevard, and became a steady customer for late breakfast at Alice's 210 Café, a restaurant a couple of blocks from the Sleeping Lady.

Sue Luna was somewhat of a maverick among Talents West dancers. Bobbie recalled her sister refused to keep her money in the safe at the club as Gilbert Pauole wanted her to, because she'd heard that dancers who did sometimes found their money gone when they'd go to get it. Besides the "table dance" fees the dancers were required to collect—a table dance was a "private" performance for a customer at the price of eight dollars—Sue would charge customers just to sit and talk. Pauole wanted a chunk of that money, but Luna refused to turn any over. All of her money was mailed to Seattle as soon as she got it.

The last time Bobbie Morehead saw Sue, they'd gone horseback riding in Chugiak. Bobbie saddled a horse named Geronimo for her sister to ride, but Sue was reluctant—she'd never been on a horse before. Bobbie assured her that the horse was very gentle.

Finally, Susie crawled up into the saddle and the sisters rode out of the corral —Bobbie riding her own horse bareback.

As luck would have it, it wasn't long before "gentle" Geronimo started rearing.

"Poor Susie," Bobbie recalled with a musing smile. "It ended up I grabbed the reins and led Geronimo back home to the corral. I think Susie was embarrassed.

"But she liked animals. I remember I gave her a puppy when she was five. Susie was a very gentle and soft-hearted person. And you know, she still sucked her thumb sometimes. . . ."

A few nights after the horseback ride, on May 24, a customer at the Good Times offered Sue Luna $300 for a photo session. She agreed to meet him at Alice's 210 the next morning around eleven. For her appointment, Sue dressed in jeans, a black and white sweater, backless high-heel shoes, and a brand new white leather jacket. Her roommate Robin handed Sue some letters to mail for her while she was out.

Robert Hansen sat in a car down the street from Alice's Café. He'd gotten everything taken care of at his bakery for the day; his help knew what to do.

He had been sitting in his parked car since around ten A.M. He was always careful to make sure he was at the rendezvous address at least half an hour ahead of time.

He'd wait where he knew his intended victim couldn't see him. If someone drove up with her and stayed—letting her out and then pulling into a parking spot and sitting there, Hansen would take off and not keep the appointment.

That morning, Robert Hansen didn't leave.

In the kitchen at Alice's, the cook glanced up from the grill and saw a woman in a white leather jacket sit down in a booth by the window. A waitress brought her order in. He'd seen her come in several mornings the past couple of weeks; she was becoming a regular.

Several minutes later the cook noticed the woman get up from her half-eaten breakfast and walk outside to a car that had just pulled up. A light-haired guy wearing glasses got out and talked with the woman. He handed her some money, and she brought it into the restaurant to pay her tab. Leaving her unfinished breakfast behind, she went back outside and got into the car as the man held the door for her.

That May morning was the last time the cook saw the attractive twenty-three-year-old strawberry blonde.

When Sue Luna didn't show up for a scheduled visit at Chugiak, Bobbie Morehead was worried. She became alarmed when her sister's roommate, Robin, told her that Sue had failed to return from a date she had with a photographer. Bobbie called the Anchorage Police Department.

The Anchorage police had been investigating the disappearances of missing dancers, and they'd discovered that many Talents West dancers were routinely shuttled on a circuit of bars that encompassed Hawaii, Seattle, Anchorage, Kodiak Island (Alaska), and some Pacific Northwest states. They suggested to Morehead that Sue might have been transferred to Hawaii or one of the other locations on the spur of the moment.

This response seemed like a brush-off to Morehead. She knew her sister would have let her know if she had to cancel their visit. Bobbie started her own investigation.

Robin told her that Sue was supposed to have met the man at Alice's 210. At the café, the cook told Bobbie what he'd seen the morning Sue disappeared. She passed that information on to the police.

While she crossed her fingers that the letters Robin gave Susie to post would show up at their destinations, Bobbie ran an ad in the paper offering a reward for any information as to the whereabouts of her sister. She got one call in response.

The voice on the phone was a man's. He spoke with a slight stutter, a hesitation. It was Robert Hansen, but he didn't identify himself. He told Bobbie he knew Susie and that she'd gone to Fairbanks with a black guy. He wanted Bobbie to meet him at a bar to talk about it.

She was reluctant to go along with the meeting because the caller said he'd known her sister a long time. But Sue Luna had been up in Alaska only a couple of weeks. Also, the cook at Alice's had told Bobbie he'd seen the strawberry blonde drive off with a white guy.

So they agreed if Susie didn't show up, Bobbie would run the ad again and he would call back. She ran it again, but he didn't call.

"Sometimes I wonder if Susie was still alive when he called and asked me to meet him," Bobbie said. "And, if I'd met him, could that have made a difference?"

Robert Hansen didn't plan to select victims that someone would aggressively search for when they disappeared. Bobbie Morehead's ad probably surprised him. He may have contacted her to find out what she knew about the circumstances surrounding her sister's disappearance; certainly, the ruse about the black man taking Sue Luna to Fairbanks was either an attempt by Hansen to throw her off the track or a ploy to see if she had a description of who'd met Sue at Alice's Café.

And there could have been another motive behind Hansen's call. Perhaps Bobbie Morehead saved her own life by refusing to meet with him.

With no other leads, Bobbie decided to go to Fairbanks to look for her sister. Susie's roommate, Robin, said she'd go along, but when Bobbie arrived at the Sleeping Lady to pick her up, Gilbert Pauole was standing by the front door. Robin came out, acting peculiar, and said she couldn't go. Bobbie elected not to go to Fairbanks by herself, and never did make the trip.

The letters Sue was to have posted for her roommate didn't arrive at their destinations, and when her six-week booking was over, Robin flew back to Seattle. Bobbie Morehead recalled: "Robin was very scared, and wanted to get out of Anchorage."

When Bobbie went to the Sleeping Lady to collect her sister's belongings, Gilbert Pauole told her that Sue had left nothing behind. Bobbie felt he was lying, but she didn't know what she could do about it.

Then the terrible waiting began. Frustration and anguish gnawed at Sue Luna's sister, and in Seattle it was the same for Sue's family and four-year-old daughter Liz.

After seeing Sergeant Haugsven at the Safeway, Bobbie Morehead didn't go straight home. Instead, she drove through Chugiak and farther up Glenn Highway to the south shoreline of the Knik River.

Parking her vehicle, she got out, walked to the edge of a bluff and looked across the expanse of the riverbed. The water level was very low; streams meandered among islands and sandbars and through protruding mounds of gray, glacial silt.

Bobbie stared across to the far side of the Knik River. For several days after Wild Cherry dancer Sherry Morrow's body was found the September before, she'd ridden her horse up and down that north bank, looking for a grave she really didn't want to find.

Chapter 16

Attorney Fred Dewey had told Robert Hansen that it appeared there was nothing to worry about as far as the Cindy Paulson case was concerned. But Hansen was shaken by his close call with the law, and restricted himself to some "polite" dating of a few more respondents to his singles ad.

By the time Mrs. Hansen and the children returned from Europe late in the summer, Robert was beginning to feel confident he'd escaped the Paulson incident completely unscathed. He retrieved the incriminating weapons he'd entrusted to John Henning back on June 13, and he put up his feet while he listened to his family tell him about their European vacation.

Then, at the end of August, he had a shock. Down in Oregon, Robert's father, Christian Hansen, had a heart attack and died. The Hansen family went down for the funeral. When they returned to Anchorage, Robert brought back his dad's gun collection.

The summer of '83 was winding down with the Labor Day weekend, and two teenage boys were spending their last vacation days moose hunting along the Knik River north of Anchorage. At 1 P.M., Friday, September 2, the two young hunters were on a sandbar about two miles upriver from the new Glenn Highway bridge, having just stepped out of some woods where they'd passed an old meat shack.

"What's this?" one of the boys blurted, confronted by the sight of several bones protruding from the sand.

The pair scrutinized what they quickly concluded to be human skeletal remains. Hurrying to a nearby cabin, they contacted authorities.

The body was eventually identified as Paula Goulding, who'd disappeared just over four months ago after leaving the Alaska Bush Company on April 24. A single .223-caliber shell casing was found mingled among her bones in the exposed grave located just a few miles from where Sherry Morrow's body had been found a year before.

Three elements appeared to link the homicides: Morrow and Goulding were both topless dancers in downtown Anchorage clubs; they were murdered by a weapon of the same caliber; and their graves were in the same general area along the Knik. Now, the term that had been casually tossed about in discussions of the

missing dancers case at the trooper station suddenly became an operative concept
—*serial killer!*

Sergeant Lyle Haugsven was on leave, hunting and fishing somewhere in the bush, when Paula Goulding's body was discovered. A decision had to be made as to who would follow up on the Goulding murder investigation to keep things moving and track a possible serial murderer.

The head of the Criminal Investigation Bureau, Lieutenant Bob Jent, was probably one of the most able and well-liked men to ever wear a commander's uniform in the Alaska State Troopers. He made assignments based on the job to be done—which trooper had the experience or record that indicated he or she was best for the task.

The job appeared to be "catch a serial killer." With that in mind, Jent pondered his command's roster, and came up with a sergeant who'd been transferred down from Fairbanks into the CIB's Narcotics Unit in Anchorage—Glenn Flothe.

Just before coming down to Anchorage, the tall, lean, and mustached Flothe had worked on a serial killer case with AST sergeant Sam Barnard. The two sergeants had used a serial killer profile provided by the Federal Bureau of Investigation's Behavioral Science Unit to track down an enlisted man, Thomas Richard Bunday, who, while stationed at Eielson Air Force Base, had murdered five Fairbanks women between 1979 and '81.

Bunday had been transferred to Wichita Falls, Texas, and an hour after a warrant for his arrest for the Fairbanks murders was issued, he committed suicide on a Texas highway by slamming his motorcycle head-on into a truck. Sergeant Flothe knew he didn't want the next killer he found to get away like that. What he didn't know was that in this new assignment, he was hunting a serial killer who would become a textbook case in serial-murder profiling.

After sending off the .223-caliber casing found in Goulding's grave for FBI testing—hopefully to confirm a match with the weapon that killed Sherry Morrow—Glenn Flothe had a lot to do. There were boxes of files and paperwork from the missing dancers cases to review—information on suspects and victims. And there were other unsolved murders of young women the sergeant had to bone up on.

In a stack of paperwork that had grown larger while Lyle Haugsven was away on leave, Flothe spied a large, sealed manila envelope. He opened it and pulled out its contents. A quick glance at a memo from an Anchorage patrolman named Gregg Baker grabbed his interest, and the sergeant flipped to an APD report: "Sexual Assault 1, File No. 83–46484, Complainant—Cindy R. Paulson."

Glenn Flothe tilted back in his chair, and with one of his index fingers, nudged his glasses up the bridge of his nose. His breathing settled to a steady, short rhythm as he reviewed the several pages of material.

How could this Robert Hansen not be one of our suspects? the sergeant thought to himself. His record . . . those assaults of women twelve years ago, now the rape charge this summer. And he was trying to fly this Cindy Paulson out to the wilderness?! . . . That's it! Goulding's grave was accessible by boat or plane, almost an impossibility on foot . . . particularly with a victim in tow.

Flothe decided that the first thing to do was gather every bit of information written down about Robert Hansen. Glenn had earned a degree in history at the University of Alaska before joining the troopers in 1974; now he would study Robert Hansen's history—he was going to get to know about this guy *from day one!*

II

from the Plains to the Rim of Fire,

Chapter 17

Esterville, Iowa, 1939

It was Wednesday, February 15, and the double feature showing at the Grand Theatre on the town square in Esterville, Iowa, was billed: "2 Ace Hits—Victor McLaglen, Chester Morris, and Wendy Barrie in PACIFIC LINER . . . They Dared to Kiss as a Terror Ship Blazed With Mutiny! and Ronald 'Dutch' Reagan and Jane Bryan in GIRLS ON PROBATION . . . Are They the Marked Women of To-morrow?"

At the Coleman Hospital, a few blocks from the town square, a son was born to Mr. and Mrs. Christian R. Hansen from nearby Armstrong. They named their firstborn Robert Christian, and when he was three years old, the Hansens moved to Richmond, California. In 1949 the Hansens returned to Iowa with their ten-year-old son and a two-year-old daughter and settled in Pocahontas, a small town 125 miles northwest of Des Moines and fifty miles south of Armstrong.

Founded in 1870 in a county with the same name, Pocahontas was one of many towns created during the rapid settlement of the flat, fertile Cornbelt after the Civil War. The town's namesake was the Virginian Indian princess whose benev-olence and interventions on behalf of the Jamestown settlers in the 1600s had made her the symbol of the American Indian welcoming Europeans to the "new world."

The basic ethnic mix of the town and its surrounding farms was established by German, Bohemian, Scandinavian, and Irish immigrants; the community's ethos evolving from the "old country" mores of hard work, temperance, religion, fru-gality, and patriarchy. The first church, St. Peter's and Paul's—built in 1875 by Bohemian Catholics—was soon followed by Lutheran, Methodist, and Presbyte-rian churches, along with a second Catholic parish (founded because of some residual "old country" bitterness between ethnic groups). The first public school opened in 1892, followed by a Catholic school in 1896.

By 1949 rural America was in the final stages of being groomed for the auto-mobile, and the Hansens' new hometown sat at the crossroads of state highways 3 and 17—later renumbered Highway 4. Pocahontas's commercial and aesthetic framework had been cemented, with its courthouse dominating the north end of a three-block main street that was paved in 1933. It had the typical businesses of a rural town—grain elevator, railroad, hotel, blacksmith, machinery and car dealers, grocery stores, produce (chicken and poultry) stores, and hardware and repair stores. On Saturday night, when the farmers and their families came into town, parking spaces were at a premium.

Pocahontas did have a few perks, including a nine-hole golf course, and a 60-by-120-foot swimming pool built by the Works Progress Administration during the Depression. And on Main Street was the Rialto Theatre, where the philosophy was: "The movie is the thing"—with television in its infancy, it was the *only thing*. There was no concession stand, and food wasn't allowed in the theatre—anyone sneaking something in would have it opened or unwrapped to avoid any crinkly noises that might expose their transgression. The best films arrived relatively soon after their release and were viewed in quiet reverence, fortified by a "cry booth" to which mothers could take their noisy infants and watch the movie from behind a glass partition.

The October 20, 1949, edition of the *Pocahontas Record Democrat* carried Moritz Motor Sales' ad for the "Kaiser Traveler—a six-passenger sedan that converts into a cargo hauler with a Cargo Hatch"—the original hatchback—"Yours for only $2,088." The competition, the Pocahontas Auto Company, listed their Ford Six Tudor Sedan "with Mid Ship Ride and Magic Action Brakes . . . all for $1,527.65." But in a large ad something was being offered for free. Mr. and Mrs. Chris Hansen announced the opening of their "Home Bakery," inviting people "to come in and get acquainted and inspect the modern bakery, and enjoy free coffee and doughnuts."

Chris Hansen had learned the baking trade in his native Denmark before immigrating to the United States at the age of twenty. He'd opened a bakery in Armstrong in 1937, and married a woman from nearby Ringsted, who joined in the business. The Hansens' move to the West Coast had not met their expectations, the lifestyle and bustle of a postwar California bay city not affording them the pace and stability of a small midwestern community. And Chris Hansen stuttered, an impediment exacerbated by his not learning to speak the English language very well. But he was a skilled baker, and a good product spoke as well as words on a small-town main street in Iowa.

At first the family lived in a small apartment above the bakery, meaning that at two A.M. work would begin, just through the door and down the stairs. The bakery prospered, the kids got bigger, and the Hansens bought a modest three-bedroom house just two or three houses from the edge of town, putting their workplace four blocks away. Acquaintances recalled that "the house was very well kept . . . always very clean. Edna was a meticulous housekeeper."

Chris Hansen was described as being a "hard-nosed authoritarian figure . . . an 'old world father,' very religious and very strict." He worked himself and his family hard, especially his only son. Robert started working around the bakery at a very early age, and his responsibilities and hours increased as he grew older, similar in many ways to what boys experienced on the surrounding family farms.

But Robert Hansen expressed resentment when he reflected on those long hours of hard work: "When I was a young boy, I worked at my dad's shop and 'd get maybe thirty-five to forty-five cents. When I got to be a sophomore, junior, senior . . . I wouldn't even get a dollar."

Like his father, Robert Hansen stuttered. Also, he was born left-handed. But his parents wanted him to be right-handed, so they pushed him to do things with his right hand. The resultant stress from that pressure may have made his speech problem worse.

During his junior high and high school days, Robert could barely control his speech at all. He said he came to hate the word "school." He would be talking to someone, trying to say something to a teacher or classmate, but wouldn't be able to get the words out. He'd walk away, humiliated.

Worst of all was when the girls made fun of him on the playground or in the halls. Perhaps if he'd been able to face their jokes and laugh along with them, their taunting him might have stopped. But he wasn't, and his subsequent feelings of rejection and inadequacy took hold of him with an anger he couldn't control.

Robert Hansen never did learn to control those feelings and anger. Ultimately, they led to his aberrant desire to control women by raping and murdering them.

Although Hansen was an average student and tested to have an IQ of 91, his scholastic performance and test scores may have been inhibited by his work schedule. A woman who taught commercial courses when Robert was in high school noticed he always seemed tired in her afternoon typing class, often falling asleep. She figured it was because he had to get up early and work in his father's bakery.

The Pocahontas community's town and rural population had peaked in the late forties, when before the advent of chemical and capital intensive methods of farming, there were about four farm families on each square mile of rich farmland. When Robert Hansen started high school in 1953, the town's population had leveled off at 2,300 people. Recreational activities for teenagers continued to expand, and a skating rink was built, eventually converted to a bowling alley. The Chief Drive-In theatre opened, where offerings of low-cost B movies combined with an abundant variety of food at the snack bar. And a completed highway system provided teenagers access to several dance halls within a forty-mile radius of Pocahontas.

Up to the mid-fifties the dance halls catered almost exclusively to adults, but with the birth of rock 'n' roll, teen dances, "hops," became a regular fixture at the ballrooms. Frequently, "dance party" tours would roll in a busload of "Top-40" stars to perform their hit songs. For $1.50 admission, the kids got to dance and watch the performances.

But Robert Hansen's workload, his strict and religious parents, and having little money at his disposal, limited his participation in social activities. Generally, he was perceived to be a "loner."

He did participate in boys' chorus, mixed chorus, and pep club at school. He took driver's ed, and even though he was heavy on the z's in typing class, he tested out at forty words per minute.

Hansen went out for basketball all four years of high school, but failed to win a letter. It was the same when he went out for football in his senior year. After four years on the track team, he finally lettered as a senior. His team events were the 880-yard and mile relays, and his individual event was the broad jump.

Still, school remained a hell for Robert. As he put it: "All through high school, if I knew there was a possibility that I would have to say anything in class or make a comment, I would literally break out in sweats, and, of course, getting excited made my stuttering worse. . . ."

Outside of school and working in the bakery, Robert pursued the more solitary activities of hunting, fishing, and archery. The outdoors provided an escape from the oven of shame he found in social situations.

On the Wednesday morning before Thanksgiving of his senior year, Robert did join his whole school and all the students from the Catholic school at the Rialto to see *War and Peace*. The screening made the movie accessible to students lacking money, time, transportation, or permission. It was one of the few times the two schools did anything together—the pre-ecumenical Catholic Church actively discouraged its youth from associating with public school students, and state law prohibited parochial school children from sharing or using the public school buses.

In May of '57 Hansen graduated with thirty-one other students in his class. Robert's name was misspelled "Hanson" in the yearbook, under which was the slogan: "Worry never made men great, so why should I worry?"

Robert continued to work in his father's bakery after graduation, then enlisted in the Army Reserves and went to basic training at Fort Dix, New Jersey.

Being away from home, and in the more cosmopolitan northeast, he discovered some new things he liked—Chinese food and Matt Helm detective stories. Also, he had his first sexual encounters.

While at Fort Dix, he was picked at random out of a chow line to be a USO "Soldier of the Week," meaning he would have an all-expense-paid weekend in New York City. When Robert told his sergeant he was going into the Big Apple, the three-striper roared to the contrary, "Bullshit, we're going on bivouac!"

But the USO prevailed. In New York, Hansen teamed up with another young soldier, and the pair decided: "Boy, while we're here, we gotta get ourselves a piece of ass." They ended up in a hotel room with two prostitutes.

The experience came up short of their expectations, however; it was just a quick jump into bed and "that was it, honey."

Robert had other encounters with prostitutes while he finished out his active-duty stint at Fort Knox, Kentucky: "On the weekends I'd go into Fort Knox, and it was strictly 'slam, bam, thank you ma'am.' "

Robert Hansen didn't like "quickies." In Alaska he would "take control of the situation" in order to avoid them.

Returning to Pocahontas on reserve status with the 103rd Military Police, he went back to work at his father's bakery. But he moved out of his parents' house and into his own apartment.

He continued to be out of the normal social mainstream, and grand jury testimony in 1961 would describe Robert as "being different," tending to associate with kids quite a bit younger than himself. "He'd have high school boys over to his apartment to talk about guns, hunting, and who or what he didn't like in Pocahontas."

Considering Robert Hansen's life up to this point, there were several elements that began to fit a serial killer profile. Hansen would develop into what the FBI classifies as an "organized serial killer"—basically, one whose crimes were well-planned and whose victims were carefully targeted strangers. The Bureau's research has found that this type of killer most likely has a high birth order—usually firstborn, good intelligence, the father's work history is stable and generally in a skilled profession, and frequently the killer has followed into that skilled trade.

Another characteristic common among organized serial killers is that they experienced inconsistent discipline in their childhood. That may have been the case for Robert Hansen. The general description of his father, one that Robert echoed himself, was that Chris Hansen was a hard-nosed, strict authoritarian. Edna Hansen may have been just the opposite, causing Robert to seek sanctuary with his mother. Studies of serial killers have shown that such a parenting situation can contribute to the development of a resentment toward women in the male child, because of his overdependence on his mother. (As a male, he resents that he is so dependent on her—thereby being deprived of his father.)

When this dynamic exists, FBI research has found another variable to be common in the childhood histories of serial rapists and killers—the denigration of the father as a male role model. Chris Hansen may have been put down as the "ornery ogre" the family had to put up with, and also ridiculed for his stuttering and not speaking English well. If this was the case, and Robert was deprived of a healthy relationship with his father while being in an overdependent one with his mother, he would have developed a more characteristically feminine egocentric personality rather than one with a "healthy" male ego. Ultimately, that would have intensified his feelings of inadequacy.

According to behavioral research, egocentrism and acute feelings of inadequacy are common to all rapists and serial killers. Particularly, it is the egocentrism that allows these criminals to discount and dehumanize their victims—the rapist or killer thinks the victim exists for their whims.

But speculation aside, Robert Hansen was an unhappy person at this point in his life, filled with a smoldering anger created by his inability to cope with the situation he perceived himself to be in. Eventually, he would act out and give a clue to his developing condition; unfortunately, neither the judicial system nor society would recognize what his first criminal act implied.

Chapter 18

In 1959 the fire department, Kiwanis, and Rotary clubs sponsored the formation of the Pocahontas Junior Police, a group to include eighth through eleventh grade boys who would be trained in first-aid, fire prevention, law enforcement, traffic control, and firearms drill. On Thursday, January 29, more than thirty youths were told about the program and sworn in. Robert Hansen was introduced by Police Chief Marvin Wiseman as one of the men who would be serving as a drill instructor.

The talks, brass, belts, and white helmets created expectations for the recruits, but some of the older cadets were thinking one day ahead to Friday night, when they would be heading to nearby Fort Dodge and the Laramar Ballroom to see the Big Bopper, Ritchie Valens, Dion and the Belmonts, and Buddy Holly and the Crickets.

Meanwhile, Robert had another new element in his social life—he started dating a girl who'd graduated a year after he did. She was the daughter of the town's chiropractor, a man who had little contact with the community outside of his practice. In fact, his whole family kept to themselves, but they belonged to the same church the Hansens did.

Hard work continued to dominate Robert Hansen's life, however.

When Police Chief Wiseman would make his early morning rounds doing the door checks on Main Street, the Hansen Bakery was one place he'd find someone else doing their job at that hour. Robert would be working there in heat that was oppressive in summer but welcome in winter. A few times Robert took Wiseman to the rear of the bakery, where he'd piled some cardboard boxes for a backstop, and showed the police chief how good he was with a bow. Wiseman appreciated Robert's archery skills—they seemed to fit with the fact that Bob was his best drill instructor for the Junior Police.

Chris Hansen decided to ease up on his workload, and hired the son of the jeweler whose shop was a few doors from the bakery. The boy was a quiet, blond, crew-cut sixteen-year-old. Robert now had someone, six years his junior, whom he could lord over and try to impress.

. . .

December 7, 1960, was the nineteenth anniversary of the bombing of Pearl Harbor. At the construction site of the new Standard Oil Station on Highway 3, it was close to quitting time, and Duane Rude was looking forward to the drive home to his farm and supper.

He looked up and saw his kids' school-bus driver, Dick Eagan, steer his car onto the site and roll down his window.

"Duane," the man hollered out, "your daughter left her trombone on my bus —I'd've brought it if I'd known you'd be here. The bus barn isn't locked, so maybe you should stop and get it. The bus is in the third stall, and the trombone is by the driver's seat."

"Thanks, Dick, I'll do that."

It was dusk when Rude closed the door on the bus stall, put the trombone in his pickup, and drove home to his farm.

Later that evening, after he finished checking the traffic and the cars parked around the Catholic school gym because of the basketball game, Police Chief Marvin Wiseman headed for the Town Pump and a hot cup of coffee. He glanced to make sure no cars were blocking the bus-barn driveway as he drove past the public school grounds.

A few minutes later, Vocational Agriculture teacher Ron Walker drove into the driveway and parked between the bus barn and the Ag Shop. In his office, he put on a pot of coffee for his students and prepared for the evening's adult Voc-Ag class.

As the coffee started to perk, Walker glanced up from his lesson plan and saw a cloudy swirl outside his office window. He went outside to check what was going on, and found smoke pouring out of the bus barn.

Police Chief Wiseman's coffee cup was half-full when he heard the fire whistle. As he raced his squad car toward Main Street, he saw smoke and flames at the bus barn, so he stopped to direct traffic at its driveway entrance.

A couple of blocks away at the Catholic school gym, the spirit of the evening was high, sweetened for the students because tomorrow was a holy day—the Feast of the Immaculate Conception—and the Catholic school would be closed. Abruptly, the basketball game was halted to announce there was a fire at the public school. Volunteer firemen ran to the exits.

With the north part of the building engulfed in flames, firemen decided there was still a possibility of saving the buses parked in the south stalls. As fireman Dutch Leonard drove one through the flames and into the clear, its gas tank exploded, throwing him from the vehicle with cuts and burns.

School custodian Earl Joachim saw what happened to Leonard, but he stayed at his task and got into another bus. When he got it out and parked at a safe distance, he leaned on the steering wheel and contemplated the smoke and flames. It gnawed his gut to know they were consuming athletic equipment, desks, stage props from class plays, tools . . . and it looked as though several buses would be destroyed.

On the south side of the barn, holding one of the hoses that wound toward the fire, was volunteer fireman Robert Hansen.

. . .

Though the Catholic school was closed the next day, there was still the usual volume of traffic for a school morning, except the cars were headed for the public school, where the academic day contended with discussion about the fire. Three buses, the barn and its contents had been destroyed; the schoolkids saw men poking around in the ashes and debris all day.

A fire marshal concluded the fire was an act of arson.

Three months of investigation produced no leads. Then Police Chief Wiseman received a call from a sixteen-year-old whose conscience was bothering him—it was the jeweler's son who worked at the Hansen Bakery.

The boy confessed that on several occasions Robert Hansen said he wanted to burn the bus barn down, to see if he could get away with it, and to get even with the school superintendent who'd disciplined him a couple of times. Finally, he'd done it.

Hansen had talked him into participating in the scheme, and on the night of the fire the two met at the bakery and quickly painted one of the ovens to establish an alibi.

They carried a five-gallon can of gasoline to the bus barn. Hansen took it up a ladder to the loft, poured the gas around, and ignited the fire. Then the pair hurried back to the bakery.

Robert Hansen was already becoming "organized." He knew the value of an alibi, and had calculated to create one. What he hadn't counted on was the basic decency of his "partner."

Charged with arson on March 29, 1961, Hansen waived a preliminary hearing and his case was bound over to a grand jury. He was jailed under $2,500 bail.

Three days later, petite Edna Hansen went to the courthouse with the bail money to get her son out of jail so he could make it to the church on time. That evening, Robert married the chiropractor's daughter in a ceremony at the Lutheran church. The newlyweds left for a week in Florida, then returned to live in Robert's apartment.

That September, Hansen was indicted for arson. In the meantime, the jeweler's son had been sent away by his family to live in Minnesota with relatives and finish out high school. In a way, he'd become Robert Hansen's first victim.

Considering the grand jury testimony and case against him, Hansen waived a trial and pleaded guilty: "I guess I burned down the bus barn because I hated the school with a divine passion. I would do whatever I could think of to get back at that monster school that did Bob Hansen a personal wrong."

Though his act of arson was clearly an assault on the community, endangering and disrupting lives, the legal system viewed it as an offense against property—an interpretation that would affect other judicial decisions concerning Robert Hansen. By the time of his conviction for rape and murder, however, "not for profit" arson would be recognized as a telltale sign of a developing sociopath—particularly of a serial rapist-killer.

On October 9, 1961, Robert was sentenced to three years at the state reformatory at Anamosa. Shortly afterward, his wife divorced him.

At Anamosa a psychiatric workup diagnosed Hansen as having "an infantile personality." This was based on Robert's description of fantasies of revenge and destruction. He revealed he imagined doing vicious things to girls who'd rejected or made fun of him, and he talked about wanting to blow up the town water tower and shoot out the lights of the town police car. "Getting even" seemed to be his obsession.

Eventually, Hansen came to the conclusion that his openness with the psychiatrists had hurt him. He had been under the impression that anything he'd tell them would be kept confidential, but things he said were thrown back at him during hearings; he missed his first chance of parole.

Robert felt they hadn't played the game fair, so he became determined never to be made "the sucker" again. He formulated a strategy he would use in the future if he got caught in a serious violation of the law. He would tell authorities that there were times when he couldn't remember his actions; that way there was a chance that he wouldn't be held responsible.

But Robert Hansen remembered everything: "I never had a period in my life when I didn't really know what was going on."

He quickly learned "to play the system" and make the best of his confinement at the reformatory. He went to work for one of the staff counselors—typing and filing records—and he wrote letters for inmates who couldn't read or write. After taking a Moody Bible Institute correspondence course, he began giving religious "counseling" to other inmates.

The counselor he worked for arranged some speech therapy for Robert at the nearby University of Iowa, and his speech gradually improved.

In late 1962 another psychiatric workup done on Hansen stated that while he still had an infantile personality, his antisocial attitudes had diminished. This report, coupled with his record of good conduct, earned him a parole on May Day, 1963.

Chapter 19

Christian Hansen was in his mid-fifties and had his own business, in a trade he'd worked at for more than thirty-five years, but it was uncomfortable to stay on the main street of a small town where everyone knew that his only son had destroyed community property and gone to jail for it. In the winter of '63 the Hansens purchased the Stony Point resort on Leech Lake, 200 miles north of Minneapolis-St. Paul, and moved up to northern Minnesota to get everything ready for the coming fishing season.

Leech Lake is surrounded by several state forests, an Indian reservation, and hundreds of little lakes which folklore contends are "the footprints of Paul Bunyan's giant blue ox Babe." In the eighteenth century the locale was an important outpost for French trappers and fur traders who gave the lake its name, Lac de la Sangsue. The area went on to become the center of a booming logging and lumber industry which spawned the Paul Bunyan legend. The "giant" lumberjack was said to have taken iron from the Mesabi Range and forged an ax with which he could cut down an acre of trees with a single blow. As fast as the forests were disappearing, this yarn was appropriate.

The lumber industry ravaged the forests and departed, but Teddy Roosevelt's conservation programs stepped in and restored the rugged, glacial moraine wilderness. The environs remained sparsely populated, and Leech Lake became a thriving outdoor resort and recreation center.

The Hansens' resort was located in the Chippewa National Forest, on a peninsula on the southwest side of the 110,000 acre lake. People came to Stony Point to fish—Leech being one of the best game-fish lakes in the United States. The resort's pamphlet promised stringers full of walleyes, muskie, northerns, bass, and "jumbo" perch; and the lake would usually deliver.

When Robert was released from Anamosa, he took his parole in Minnesota and went to work at his parents' resort, spending the first weeks helping paint the boats and cabins and putting out the docks. When the season began, he guided fishing parties. He liked his new, wilderness environment.

And that summer he met his second wife. She was one of the girls his folks had hired to clean the cabins. She came from Iowa; her parents ran the motel in Pocahontas.

Gloria Deacon and her family had moved to Pocahontas in 1960, when she was a junior in high school. Being almost five-foot-eleven, she promptly made the girls' basketball team, as well as the softball team. She participated in a lot of extracurricular activities, did well in high school, and was attending the University of Iowa. She came to Stony Point that summer to earn some money for her sophomore year.

Robert and Gloria saw a lot of each other at the resort. When he proposed at the end of the summer, she said yes. They planned to marry when she finished college.

Gloria went back to Iowa U. that fall. Robert completed a three-and-a-half week short course at the Wilton School of Cake Decorating in Chicago, then returned to his parents' resort.

For a while the couple wrote to each other, and Robert made the long drive down to Iowa City to see her a few times. But he got tired of those long trips, so the two talked it over and decided to get married—Gloria would complete her degree at the University of Minnesota, and he would get a job in Minneapolis. That was their initial plan.

But a friend of Robert's folks was staying at their resort, and he let it be known that his brother had a bakery in Minot, North Dakota, that he was having problems with, and that his brother needed a baker to run it. Chris Hansen volunteered his son for the job.

Robert grudgingly took the job, but he and Gloria got married after he'd been in Minot a month. However, he had trouble on the job, and in a few weeks they returned to the Stony Point resort.

Then Hansen was hired by the Cox Bakeries, and the couple moved to Moorhead, Minnesota. Robert was supposed to rotate among the bakery chain's thirty-two shops scattered throughout the Midwest, filling in for the regular managers while they took their vacations. His first assignment was a two-week stint in Rapid City, South Dakota.

So Hansen faced what many young men starting a new marriage and job do—having to travel and be away from home a lot. When he got back from Rapid City, he and Gloria decided they didn't like the situation and would go back to their original plan and move to Minneapolis.

After having bounced around for several months, the couple now stayed in one spot for a while. They lived at the Collins Trailer Park on East Seventy-eighth Street in the suburb of Bloomington. Gloria attended the University of Minnesota, and Robert worked at the Myhr Bakery in uptown Minneapolis, on West Fiftieth.

Robert was hired as a foreman and cake decorator. His employer found him to be an excellent worker, though sometimes he blew his top at people working under his supervision. He was always polite to his boss, however, as he was to anyone who held authority over him.

The bakery owner recalled that in over two years, he never did meet Robert's parents, and as far as he knew, Hansen didn't associate with them much. He remembered talking to them once on the phone; they called the bakery to talk to Bob because he didn't have a phone in his trailer. "They didn't say much, but they both went out of their way to tell me he was 'a good boy.' Maybe they thought I needed reassurance about him."

And maybe the bakery owner did. Robert was hiding all sorts of radios, small appliances, and sporting goods around the shop. Everyone figured it was stolen merchandise. Since Hansen's wife was religious and a "good woman," they supposed Robert was hiding the stuff at the bakery because there was no way for him to conceal it in his small trailer, where his wife would find it and know what he was up to.

Once, one of the baker's employees took his boss outside to have a look in Hansen's car. In the backseat were two bicycles—padlocks still on the wheels. Apparently, Robert had stolen them on the way to work in the morning darkness.

On February 22, 1965, a Bloomington policeman arrested Robert Hansen for stealing some fish line and lures worth eleven dollars from a sporting goods store. Not wanting his wife to find out, Robert called his employer to bail him out.

She found out, however, but being a dutiful wife, Gloria Hansen persuaded their Lutheran pastor to vouch for Bob, and the charges were dropped.

A couple of months later, Robert's employer came into the shop early and found his foreman had broken into the office by using a knife on the lock. Hansen was rifling the desk drawer where the cash for change was kept.

The baker was infuriated: "That was it! I called the county attorney about pressing charges. But then Bob came to me and said he'd been offered more money to work at the Northside Bakery. That simplified things—I told him to go ahead and take the job."

That May, Robert was arrested at a Montgomery Ward store for stealing a softball. Though he'd had no history of theft on the main street of his Iowa hometown, in Minneapolis his kleptomania seemed to explode. His thievery was in good part thrill-seeking, and he'd bragged to the other employees at the Myhr Bakery how he would go into a store and try on a suit, then walk out of the store wearing it.

Like his act of "not-for-profit" arson, Hansen's senseless stealing was another signal of his developing sociopathic personality. Kleptomania is in the history of most rapists and serial killers.

In the spring of '67 Gloria was looking forward to graduating from the university, and it was time to move on. Both she and Robert liked the wilderness that surrounded Leech Lake, so they knew they wanted to live in the wide-open spaces. But not in Minnesota. They decided on Alaska.

In June the couple stuffed their belongings and a tent into a new Pontiac and headed for the Pacific Northwest—angling through national parks and camping along the way. They stayed in the Grand Teton National Park to take mountain-climbing lessons, then drove north to enjoy the beauty of Glacier National Park.

Arriving in Vancouver, they discovered it necessary to reserve well in advance if you wanted to get your vehicle onto one of the ferries that sail up to Alaska's coastal harbors. They headed back eastward to Highway 97, and then up to catch the Alcan Highway north to Alaska.

In the fall there are some nights the Alcan can be driven without headlights—the roadway illuminated by a panorama of aurora borealis (northern lights) and moonlight. On the Hansens' summer trip, there were extra-long days which should have afforded them the opportunity to enjoy the scenery, but to their disappointment, it rained day after day.

They drove out of the Yukon and into Alaska, arriving in Anchorage in mid-August.

Chapter 20

Alaska's 591,004-square-mile area equals one third of the lower forty-eight states' combined land area. Its 1967 population was 278,000—a perspective of that population to Alaska's size is to consider Manhattan Island having only eleven people living on it.

Anchorage is located in south-central Alaska at the northeastern end of the Cook Inlet Basin, a 37,000-square-mile area shaped in a horseshoe by a quintet of mountain ranges. On the west, the Aleutian Range extends 160 miles to the north to overlap with the Alaska Range as it curves across the top of the basin. On the east, the Talkeetna Mountains go from the Alaska Range to the Matanuska River Valley. Across that valley the Chugach Range stretches to the southwest along the Gulf of Alaska coast to the Kenai Mountains, which buttress the basin from the rough gulf waters on the south and the tides of Cook Inlet on the north.

Anchorage's municipality covers a 2,000-square-mile triangular lowland, bounded on the northwest, west, and southwest by the Knik and Turnagain arms, and on the east by the Chugach Mountains. Sixty percent of its land area is comprised of Chugach State Park and National Forest, and most of its population is concentrated in a 126-square-mile area called the Anchorage Bowl.

The town came into existence in 1915, when President Woodrow Wilson proposed a rail route to connect the interior coal fields of the Matanuska and Nenana valleys to the ice-free port of Seward, Alaska. Anchorage was the staging area for the project, and overnight a tent city of two thousand railroad workers and a handful of merchants sprouted up. A chaos of mud, men, and mules quickly pushed the settlement to form a town.

On July 10, 1915, there was an auction of 655 town-site lots, the land comprising today's Fourth Avenue area in Anchorage. The price range for the lots ended up going from $75 to $1,100 apiece. Ironically, there was a stipulation that the purchaser was bound to follow: "[The lots] are not to be used for the sale of liquor, gambling or immoral purposes. Violation means forfeiture of property." Wide concrete sidewalks were poured on Fourth Avenue in 1916, and it was designated as the central business area.

By 1940 Anchorage had doubled its original population, and with the arrival of Fort Richardson and Elmendorf Air Force Base, it expanded sixfold to 30,000 people by 1950, making it the largest city in the territory. Construction of an international airport to go with its port and railroad ensured Anchorage's future as the hub for the economic development of Alaska. Also, it had Merrill Field, on its way to becoming one of the busiest private-plane airstrips in the world.

In 1964 south-central Alaska was hit by the greatest recorded earthquake ever to strike the North American continent. Anchorage shook for five minutes as the quake reached 9.2 on the Richter scale.

The city survived much better than many other coastal towns because it sat at the top of Cook Inlet and was sheltered from the ensuing tidal wave, or "tsunami". The Fourth Avenue Movie Theatre and its handsome woodwork and bronze and silver murals stayed intact, as did the fourteen-story McKinley Building—soon to be auctioned off and renamed the Mackay Building. But much of downtown Anchorage had to be rebuilt.

Reconstruction was quickly accomplished, and expansion continued. In 1967 Anchorage's 108,000 people was thirty-nine percent of the state's population, and in the next fifteen years its number of city residents would double.

The Hansens arrived in Anchorage and had no trouble finding employment in a job market hungry for persons with a trade or degree. Robert went to work as a baker and cake decorator for the Safeway Bakery at Ninth and Gambell, and Gloria got a job teaching on Government Hill.

They rented an apartment by the Safeway, then another on Dawson Street. After a year of renting, motivated by the income-tax bite on a dual income, they bought a duplex on Sixth Avenue in South Mountain View, where they lived in one half and rented out the other.

Mrs. Hansen became active in the Lutheran Central Church, and she and Robert went hiking, camping, climbing, and fishing together. Robert threw himself into archery and bow hunting, and joined the Black Sheep Bowmen and the Alaska Archery Association.

In 1969 Hansen got into the Pope and Young record book twice, shooting a fourth-ranked mountain goat on the Kenai Peninsula, and bringing down a thirty-third-ranked Barren Ground caribou along the Tyonne River.

In 1970 he bagged a Dall sheep that ranked third. When the trophy was assessed for the Pope and Young record book, Robert met John Sumrall, who was there to witness the measurement, and the two became friends and hunting buddies.

The following year was eventful for both Robert and Gloria, as they prepared for the arrival of their first child. They sold their duplex at a substantial profit and moved a few blocks north to a larger house on Thomas Circle, and Robert took a second job at another bakery.

The Hansens had a baby girl. At her baptism at Lutheran Central Church, family friend Gerald Goldschmidt was a sponsor.

With the pregnancy and parenthood, the Hansens began to go their separate ways, no longer going on wilderness outings together. As a couple, they continued to participate in church and social functions.

In 1971 Robert brought down the biggest Dall sheep ever taken by a bow.

Controversy surrounded the world record kill, including allegations that the sheep was taken in an area closed to hunting, and another that it was killed with the help of a firearm. But Hansen signed the Pope and Young "Fair Chase Affidavit," wherein he swore no firearm was used, and John Sumrall vouched to the kill.

Hansen also bagged the second-ranked Barren Ground caribou that year. But the 1970–71 recording period would be the last time he would enter a record into Pope and Young. He began to collect other "trophies."

Chapter 21

November 15, 1971

Susie Heppeard had spent a hectic Sunday taking calls at her reception desk at an Anchorage realty office. She was eighteen years old, and it was her first job. Happy it was now Monday, her day off, she'd spent the morning shopping and was driving home to relax.

On Northern Lights Boulevard she stopped at a red light, and in a casual pan her eyes met those of a man in a car next to her. She gave a reflex smile, the light changed, and she drove home to an apartment she shared with two roommates in the Spenard section of Anchorage.

After trudging up two flights of stairs with her shopping bags and entering her apartment, Heppeard decided to shower before unpacking her purchases. Just as she was about to step under a soothing spray of warm water, there was a knock at the door. She grabbed a towel and went to answer it.

Opening the door, she was confronted by the man she'd seen in the car next to her at the stoplight.

Beneath a fluorescent orange cap two eyes gawked through a pair of glasses at the woman who was holding a towel in front of her naked body. At the stoplight, Robert Hansen had taken her smile as approval.

He pretended he was trying to find someone in the apartment complex. "Ah, well, maybe could I see your phone book a second?"

It was on the table by the door; Heppeard let him look.

"Hmmm, must be unlisted." Hansen stayed with his charade, then tried to start a conversation. He told the young woman he was new in Anchorage, didn't know many people, would she like to go out with him on a date?

"No thanks," Susie said. "I'm engaged."

Hansen left. His casual approach hadn't worked.

The following Monday, Heppeard left her apartment at five-fifteen A.M. to drive some friends to work. She dropped them off, then drove back home, unaware that someone was waiting in the darkness.

As her car's headlight beams swept across the yard when she turned into the driveway, Susie saw a man in an orange cap hurry behind a neighboring building. She parked her car in the carport and got out.

Suddenly, the man in the orange cap stepped in front of her and pointed a gun in her face.

"Shut up, sweetheart, or I'll blow your brains out!" he snarled.

Heppeard screamed.

Her assailant cocked the revolver and scowled, "Scream again and I'll blow your head off!"

Susan Scott was in a back bedroom ironing a blouse when she heard a scream outside. She hurried into the living room and looked out the window. She saw a man standing with her roommate in the lighted area at the base of the stairway, and it looked like the man might be holding a gun.

Anxiously, Scott opened the door and called down, "What's going on, Susie? Are you all right?"

Getting no reply, Scott quickly closed the door and telephoned the police. While she was on the phone, a sleepy Frances Lake joined her by the front window.

"That's right, officer, 3608 Lois Drive . . . hurry!"

"What's going on?" Lake said, blinking the sleep out of her eyes. "I thought I heard a scream."

"You did. Down there—I think that guy may be going to rape Susie!"

Frances Lake quit blinking and stared through the window.

The women could see that the man was holding a gun to their friend's head. The guy was wearing a bulky, green army jacket over a plaid shirt, and his orange cap covered what appeared to be blond hair.

Lake, scared and angry, stuck her head out the door and yelled, "Susie, get away from that jerk! We've called the police!"

The man pushed the gun into Heppeard's back and walked her toward the street. Suddenly, he stopped, looked around in an apprehensive manner, and walked off into the darkness by himself.

Hearing the sound of an approaching siren, Lake began flicking a switch to flash the outside light over their apartment door.

APD officers Greg Frank and Archie Hutchinson were answering the call from Dispatch: ". . . possible rape in progress with weapon involved." They'd pushed it with lights and siren, and as they sped up to 3608 Lois Drive, they could see a bulb flashing on the third floor.

Heppeard saw the officers scramble out of their patrol car with guns drawn. Her feeling of relief turned back to fear of being shot, and she dropped to the ground shrieking, "He said he was going to blow my head off!"

The police started combing the area around the apartment building, and a backup unit that included Patrolman William Dennis arrived to join the search.

The terrified Heppeard hugged the ground, her face buried in the snow. When she was confident there wasn't going to be any shooting, she got up and ran to her apartment.

Still shaking, Susie Heppeard told the policemen about the gun and the threats, ". . . then he said we're going someplace we can be alone, but when he heard the sirens, he took off."

After getting a description of the suspect and his attire, Officer Hutchinson hurried out and gave the information to Patrolman Dennis and the other officers, and a search began.

At seven A.M. Hutchinson spotted a man walking through the snow and darkness in plaid shirtsleeves. Cautiously approaching in his squad car, he could see the man was wearing glasses.

"Halt! Anchorage police!"

"Sure, Officer. What's going on?" Hansen identified himself, told Hutchinson he'd been driving and felt woozy, so he'd pulled over and started walking to get some fresh air.

Back at the apartment complex, Heppeard looked through the window at Hansen slouching in the backseat of the squad car. "That's him!"

Another patrol car pulled up; Hansen's vehicle had been located, and a loaded .22-caliber pistol had been found under the driver's seat. Another officer had found an orange cap in the snow, and a .357 Magnum revolver on the top of a tire in the rear wheelwell of an abandoned Chevy.

At eight A.M. Hansen was interviewed at APD headquarters. He told officers he'd planned to go out by the Anchorage International Airport that morning to hunt moose with a bow, but he needed to get a permit at the Fish and Game Office first. Since it had been too early for the office to be open, he'd ended up driving around the Spenard area to kill time.

The orange cap and .357 Magnum were shown to the suspect, and he acknowledged their similarity to ones he owned.

Hansen repeated what he'd told officers at the scene—that he'd felt woozy and had a blackout of memory. Finally, he admitted he could have been involved in the incident that Heppeard described, but had no memory of it. "If I was, I need help," he said.

At police headquarters Heppeard and her roommates individually viewed a seven-man lineup, and each identified "number four"—Robert Hansen—as Susie's assailant.

A sample of Hansen's hair, his boots, orange cap, and .357 Magnum revolver were sent to the FBI for testing, and Robert was booked for assault with a deadly weapon.

On December 2 a preliminary hearing on the charge was held in Superior Court. Five witnesses testified—two police officers, Susie Heppeard, and her *former* roommates. Terrified by the incident, Frances Lake had moved to West Sixteenth Street, and Susan Scott to North Klevin Street.

Defense attorney James Gilmore requested to submit an order that his client be examined at the Langdon Psychiatric Clinic, and that he be released on his own recognizance.

The prosecutor objected, saying since the defendant had threatened the life of Susan Heppeard, bail should be set at $2,000.

Gilmore countered, pointing out Hansen was in the eighth year of a marriage, had a child, and owned property in Anchorage—the profile of "a well-respected man".

Robert was released on his own recognizance, with the condition he have no contact whatsoever with Susan Heppeard. That stipulation did very little to allay Susie's fears.

Two weeks later a grand jury charged Hansen with assault with a deadly weapon. A court order was entered that he be examined by psychiatrist Dr. Ray Langdon. The defendant's release would continue under the same stipulations, and proceedings in the case were scheduled to resume in January.

Hansen went to see Dr. Langdon at four that afternoon.

Chapter 22

Six days before Christmas, Anchorage Sunday shoppers could expect less than six hours of daylight in which to scurry between shops and malls. But at four A.M., eighteen-year-old Barbara Fields was getting into her car and looking forward to sleeping through most of that daylight.

As she began her trek home to P Street, the windshield of her ice-cold car fogged up. Shivering, she stretched in an arch over the steering wheel to clear a porthole with her glove, then watched as her breath floated to the glass to undo her effort.

On Gambell Street she spotted the Nevada Café. With the thought of a hot cup of tea in mind, Barbara pulled into its parking lot.

Hunched over in the warmth of the black leather coat her father had given her, she trotted inside to the counter and ordered some tea. She loosened her wrap, and as she began to feel the warmth of the café, it dawned on her she would have to return to a freezing car. She got up.

"Look," Fields said to the black waitress heading toward her with a steaming cup, "I'll be right back—I'm going out to start my car so it can warm up."

The waitress gave her a glazed, four A.M. nod of approval.

Getting into her car, Barbara saw a silver-blue Pontiac pull in next to her and was vaguely aware of a man getting out of the vehicle as she started her car. Confident of the idle, she got out and headed for her tea, noticing that the man had stopped outside the café door.

The man attempted to start a conversation, but Fields brushed him off.

He moved quickly to block her path. "Look, maybe you and I . . ." There was a slight hesitation in his speech.

When Barbara tried to brush him off again and push by him, the man reached into his coat pocket and pulled a gun. "Now, you listen and do what I say . . . don't scream."

Terrified, Fields thought only about the gun pushed in her back as she was steered to the Pontiac and into its front seat.

As the car pulled out onto Gambell and headed south, Barbara looked toward her captor—the glow of the dashlights revealed he had a pockmarked face.

Taking Fireweed Lane, then heading south again on Arctic Boulevard, they met a police car.

"There goes your help," the man smirked to Barbara, the reflection in his glasses obscuring the threat of his eyes. "Look, if we do get stopped by the cops, don't do or say anything, or I'll have to shoot them." Robert Hansen hit her. "Understand?"

The woman shook in a frightened, staccato nod.

"I'm going to tie you up." Hansen pulled over and took some leather shoelaces out of his coat pocket. He made his captive kneel in front of the dashboard while he bound her wrists behind her back.

"It's too tight!" Fields half-cried.

Hansen hit her. "Shut up!" He moved her back into the seat and bound her ankles, drawing the lace tight around Barbara's knee-high black leather boots, his gaze lingering on her legs, exposed below her miniskirt.

Driving on across Campbell Creek, Hansen cut a left onto Dimond Boulevard, then a right onto the Seward Highway to head for the Kenai Peninsula.

Outside Anchorage, along the Turnagain Arm, Barbara started to feel the strain of her bonds and the slumping posture they forced her to maintain. Despite her fearful situation, she had the spunk to complain. "Look, I can't sit this way much longer."

She got a scowling glance.

"Couldn't you tie my hands in front of me?" she asked.

"No." He pulled the car over at a gravel pit. "You'll go in back."

With his captive lying on a blanket in the backseat, he drove on.

Just below Barbara's face on the floor in the back was a hammer. She wished her hands weren't bound so she could pick it up and smash her abductor's head with it. But then she started thinking that could kill him, which would make her a murderer, and that ran against her Christian upbringing.

Hansen turned onto Indian Road, drove to its dead-end, turned the car around and stopped. He leaned over the back of the driver's seat and leered, his eyes becoming fixed on Barbara's disheveled blouse, which revealed some black lace on her bra.

To her surprise, in a very calm and polite manner he asked her if he could rip off her bra.

She said that she wished he wouldn't, because it was brand-new and had cost her a lot of money.

Instead of ripping it off, he untied her hands. "Take off your dress and bra— you won't run if you're naked."

Fields complied. Staying calm, she asked if he had any cigarettes. Leering silence the only answer she got, Barbara asked, "Look, could we get some?"

Hansen blinked out of his stare. For some reason, he decided to accommodate his captive. "You've been doing what you're told . . . I'll get you some at Portage." He let Barbara put on her coat, then tied her wrists to the door handle.

At the café at Portage Glacier, Hansen parked away from its entrance and ran in for the cigarettes. Bound to the door handle, Barbara didn't budge until he returned with them. He released her so she could have a smoke, and when she was done, he laid her down on the backseat with her hands tied behind her and continued on to the Kenai Peninsula.

Eighty miles from Anchorage, Hansen took Highway 1 west toward Cooper Landing. Barbara was startled out of a daze as he suddenly pulled off on a side road and into an open field.

He stopped the car and reached over the seat to untie her ankles. "Sit up." He freed her hands. "Now, get up front and take the rest of your clothes off." His voice was deliberate and threatening.

Scared and resigned, Fields complied. She swallowed her loathing while her captor kissed and fondled her.

After about fifteen minutes he had her put on her underwear, nylons, boots, and coat, then bound her hands. Driving west a few miles, Hansen pulled in at the Kenai Lodge to rent a cabin. None available, he drove east, recalling that they'd passed the Sunrise Inn. Stopping at a rest area, he retied Barbara's hands to the door handle, then hit her. "Now, at this next place, don't cause any trouble or people will get hurt!"

At the Sunrise, he parked well away from the office, took off his glasses, pulled a knit cap low over his face, and went in and rented a room. His car in front of room number 4, he freed his victim from the door handle, draped her dress over her wrists to conceal their bondage, untied her ankles, and handed her purse to her.

"Listen, don't goof up. I'd hate to have to kill someone."

As soon as they were in the room, Fields asked if she could go to the bathroom.

"Wait," said Hansen. He went into the bathroom, saw the window was frozen shut and there were no objects his victim could use as a weapon, then told her to go ahead, but to leave the door open.

Barbara said she was cold and wanted to take a hot bath—she was trying to put off the inevitable. Hansen said all right, but to keep the door open. He sat at the foot of the bed and stared into the bathroom while she bathed.

When she finished, he tied her to the bed post, then took his clothes off and went into the bathroom.

Barbara noticed that when he undressed he was aroused and "ready to go," but there was something weird—the end of his penis was either deformed or mutilated. She knew the difference between circumcised and not.

She heard him run some water in the tub and splash it around; she didn't think he actually got in. He came out after about ten minutes and got into bed.

He forced her to have sex with him, threatening her several times. "Try harder, or I'll put you in the hospital."

Finished, he tied her up again and slept for an hour. Awakening, he had her put on her coat and they went out to the car and headed back toward Anchorage.

Just as Barbara was beginning to feel she was going to be allowed to survive the ordeal, Hansen made a U-turn and headed back toward the Kenai.

"Why are we going this way?" she asked timidly.

Her captor told her he wanted to look at a cabin he'd taken some girl to the weekend before.

Serial rapists and killers frequently go back to the scenes of assaults as a turn-on to "relive" the excitement. Also, to accomplish the same thing, they keep "souvenirs" of their victims—articles of clothing, jewelry, sometimes even body parts. Hansen's "unique" souvenir would be his aviation map covered with asterisks.

But a heavy snowfall denied Hansen his pleasure. Going up the mountains on Cooper Lake Road, the roadway became impassable.

Irritation registered on his pockmarked face as he turned the car around. He tied his captive's hands again and got out his gun.

Barbara's fears intensified as they drove down the mountain, Hansen gazing off the side of the bank. She felt he was stewing about what to do with her, maybe shoot her and throw her off the cliff.

Twenty years later she had a vivid memory of what happened next, things that to her were so embarrassing at the time, she never did tell her family or the court:

> Suddenly, he stopped the car, and we got out. He cocked his gun and told me, "Start running."
>
> Well, I wasn't going to run and get shot in the back. I dropped to my knees and begged and pleaded . . . said I wasn't going to run, no matter what.
>
> I said anything that I thought might save my life. I told him he was handsome, that he was good in bed, that we could date. I pleaded with him that I didn't want my baby son to lose his mother.

Apparently, something she said finally broke through to Hansen. Of course, he may just have wanted her to squirm. Whatever, he seemed to equivocate, but said he couldn't let her go because she'd turn him in to the police.

She pointed out that she'd cooperated up to that point, and assured him she wouldn't call the police. She told him to get her name and address as a kind of insurance. "Look in my purse for my license."

But Barbara wanted to take back those words as soon as she'd said them. Some of her dad's business cards were in her purse, and he was a State Trooper. She felt sure that Hansen would kill her if he found out her dad was a cop.

He didn't run across one of those cards, but did find some papers that said her parents had custody of her son until she could support him. He wrote down their names and address on a piece of paper and put it in his wallet. He put his captive back in the car and headed for Anchorage.

The sun was low in the south behind a fine mist when they reached Portage— the glacier had an ethereal blue glow. Hansen stopped at the café to buy some soda and candy, then drove on. The rest of the way he kept threatening Barbara that if she did go to the police, he would hurt her baby or her parents.

They got back to Anchorage around two P.M. Hansen left his victim a block from the Nevada Café and drove off.

Fields walked to her car; it wouldn't start because it had idled itself out of gas. She telephoned her father and, fighting back tears, described what had happened. He told her to hold tight, he and her brother would come to get her.

Barbara Fields had escaped with her life, perhaps because she'd kept her cool and had been somewhat assertive, without being confrontational, with Hansen. Given his desire "to look at a cabin," apparently there'd been at least one other victim between Heppeard and the State Trooper's daughter, and the fact his penis was mutilated meant there was a good chance he associated violence with sex. At this point Robert Hansen's aberrant hunt was well under way, and the implications were it could become more violent.

Because of her assailant's insidious threats, Barbara Fields didn't tell anyone outside her family what Hansen had done to her. She told them only part of the story; some of the details were too painful. But three days after she was kidnapped and assaulted, something happened that made her change her mind and ignore her apprehensions.

Around nine P.M. on December 22, Celia VanZanten left her family's house on Knik Avenue to get some soda at a store on Northern Lights Boulevard. The petite blonde, a freshman at Anchorage Community College, didn't return home, but her family didn't worry—they assumed she'd gone from the store to a baby-sitting job.

The next morning, Celia's bedroom door stayed closed. Everyone in the house figured she was sleeping late; she'd come home after everybody else had gone to bed, they thought. Finally, at noon, they checked and discovered that her bed hadn't been slept in. Their concern growing, they called the people whom they thought Celia babysat for and found out the sitting job had been canceled.

Celia's father contacted the Anchorage police to report her missing.

Two days later, twenty-two-year-old John Korpi and his younger brother, nineteen-year-old James, were twenty miles south of Anchorage at the McHugh Creek Campgrounds just off Seward Highway, trying out new cameras they'd received for Christmas that morning.

James walked down to the creek, forty feet below the campground, to take some pictures of ice formations. He noticed something about halfway up the slope of the ravine, and called to his brother.

"It looked like a mannequin," they told state troopers later. It was the partially-clad, frozen body of Celia VanZanten. Her hands were tied behind her back.

As the tragedy was headlined in Anchorage newspapers on December 27, troopers awaited an autopsy report. They suspected the victim hadn't been dead when she was thrown into the ravine; that she'd attempted to climb the steep slope but couldn't make it with her hands tied behind her. Late in the day the autopsy confirmed that VanZanten had died of exposure.

When Barbara Fields read about the VanZanten murder, she went to State Trooper headquarters to press charges against Hansen. "I knew I had to do something," she said. "If he was the one who murdered her, I should've had him arrested before he could do it."

It's not unusual for victims of rape to conjure up feelings of guilt; the source can be the assault itself, or other peripheral circumstances. There are also "secondary" victims—spouses, relatives, persons close to the victim—to whom a specter of guilt may appear. Fields sensed that with her father:

> I know the whole thing was very difficult for my dad to deal with. All his adult life he'd been protecting people—he was a good cop. Then his daughter, "all sugar and spice and so on," gets hurt . . . "she wasn't protected."
>
> And being a Christian, I'm sure he was ashamed of the anger it all caused in him. He shouldn't have, but I know he blamed himself. And even now, twenty years later, I'm afraid he still can't really talk about it.

After giving her statement at trooper headquarters, Fields accompanied AST sergeant Donald Hughes on the route Hansen had taken to the Kenai. At the Sunrise Inn the sergeant verified that Robert Hansen had rented a room there on December 19.

It was a difficult trip for Barbara to make. Sergeant Hughes was a friend of her father's, she knew he was a good person, and he was being very nice to her. But it was very uncomfortable for her to be alone with a man on that route, and she wished a woman were with them. As they drove along, she felt herself shrinking toward the car door, pressing up against it.

Back in Anchorage, Hughes and other troopers put Hansen under arrest. They asked him to display the contents of his wallet, and they saw the piece of paper Barbara had told Hughes contained her son's and parents' names and address in Hansen's handwriting.

At the jail, the booking officer was told there was evidence in the prisoner's wallet, and that someone would be returning with a warrant to seize it. During the booking process, Hansen was spotted attempting to remove the incriminating paper from his wallet, so the duty officer took him away for a shakedown. The search produced the piece of paper, all crumpled up in the pocket of the suspect's coveralls.

"What's this?" the officer asked.

"The people who're gonna raise my bail," Hansen answered.

The duty officer didn't understand the evidentiary value of the piece of paper, and failed to preserve it. Instead, he copied the names and addresses onto another piece of paper and put the copied information into the case file envelope. When troopers returned with a warrant to seize the contents of Hansen's wallet, the original piece of paper containing Robert's handwriting couldn't be found.

On December 29 Hansen was arraigned and held on $50,000 bail. On page two of its afternoon edition that day, the *Anchorage Times* reported the charges against him, noting also the court action pending in the Heppeard case and the fact that Hansen had been at-large on his own recognizance at the time of this second offense.

Right above the report was a short, ten-line article with the headline: CELIA VANZANTEN FUNERAL IS HELD.

Chapter 23

The history of the adjudication of rape indicates that it's not the circumstantial evidence, but the victim's background that usually has the greatest impact on the outcome of a case. Defense lawyers attempt to bring out or imply nonconformist behavior or misconduct in a plaintiff's history, hoping that a judge or jury will infer that in some way the victim consented to the assault—the "she asked for it" defense. The shopping list of negative behavior includes such things as not reporting the assault immediately, sleeping with a boyfriend, suspicion or allegation of prostitution, working as a dancer in a bar, a criminal record, having an "illegitimate" child, involvement with drugs, accepting a ride from a stranger or hitchhiking, walking alone at night, drinking alone in a bar, or even just wearing a miniskirt.

On January 7, 1972, rapist Robert Hansen faced his accuser, Barbara Fields, in a preliminary hearing. Before the court and an audience which included witnesses for the defense, she identified Hansen as her assailant and calmly told the story of how he kidnapped and raped her at gunpoint. When Prosecutor Justin Ripley finished questioning her, the attorney for the defense, James Gilmore, began his cross-examination.

Asked when and where she worked last, Barbara replied it was about a month ago, as a dancer at a bar called the Embers.

Gilmore asked her if she had to pay rent to live at her parents' house, and she said no.

"Did you or do you have any other sources of income?" he asked.

"No, I don't," Fields responded.

"Did you ever work as a prostitute?"

"No."

"Never propositioned anyone?"

The prosecutor wasn't objecting to Gilmore's line of questioning.

"No, I never propositioned anyone," Fields answered.

"Miss Fields, how long have you lived up here?"

"All my life."

"And are you related to any law enforcement officer?"

"Yes, my father is a State Trooper."

"And Miss Fields, are you . . . have you ever been married?"

"No."

"Do you have any children?"

Barbara answered yes, and Gilmore made her explain that her parents had custody of her son because she wasn't in a position to support him.

Gilmore questioned the plaintiff about drug use. She acknowledged some experimentation with heroin, but never any addiction, and she hadn't used any for quite some time.

Then the defense attorney began a vigorous series of questions that required Barbara to describe the event of December 19 in great detail. In repeated attempts to fluster her, he jumped back in the chronology of her story to ask for a diagram or for her to recall a specific detail: Did you say right or left turn? . . . Which hand was the gun in? . . . Was it five A.M. or six? But Fields was unflappable; she brushed off Gilmore's strategy and stuck to her story.

When he asked why she'd waited a week to report the incident, she said she reported it because she read about the girl being murdered at McHugh Creek. Asked if her father had brought the matter to police attention, she said she didn't know.

Gilmore circled back to the veiled innuendo he'd pursued at the beginning of the cross-examination, dwelling on what Fields wore on December 19—a floral miniskirt, knee-high black leather boots, and leather coat. His last questions were about the rape:

"When you were having intercourse, was he on top, or you?"

"He was."

"Were you having a menstrual period at the time?"

"No."

Barbara Fields was the only witness for the prosecution. AST sergeant Donald Hughes was subpoenaed to testify but didn't appear. There was no testimony to corroborate Fields's story, and the existence and disappearance of the piece of paper containing her baby's and parents' names in Hansen's handwriting weren't established for the record or the spectators in the courtroom.

After lunch, proceedings resumed before a different judge to consider a reduction of Hansen's $50,000 bail. There were three witnesses for the defense, two of whom had heard the plaintiff testify that morning. Gilmore called his first witness, the Reverend Albert L. Abrahamson, pastor of Lutheran Central Church, and began questioning.

"Mr. Hansen has the reputation of being a peaceable man?"

"As far as anything I've heard, his reputation is good," the cleric answered.

"Are you aware that he has two charges pending against him, and one of those is what we're discussing here today, a kidnap-rape charge? You saw and heard the complaining witness testify this morning. . . . Did any of that change your opinion of Mr. Hansen's character in any way?"

The reverend's strong, pulpit-trained voice seemed to get louder as he expressed confusion over just what Gilmore was asking him. Maybe at this point he was beginning to feel uncomfortable about vouching for Hansen.

A mild semantic duel broke out between the defense attorney and the minister,

Robert Hanson
"Hans"

"Worry never made man great so why should I worry."

Pep Club 3,4; Football 4; Basketball 1,2,3,4; Track 1,2,3, lettered 4; Mixed Chorus 2,3,4; Boys Chorus 3,4, Typing 40 wpm; Driver Education 2.

Robert Hansen's high school yearbook picture, 1957.
He was upset that his name was misspelled.

Robert Hansen's Super Cub, the bush plane he used to transport his victims from Anchorage to the Alaskan wilderness. *(Courtesy Alaska State Troopers)*

A portion of Robert Hansen's arsenal discovered in his attic by state troopers, including the Ruger mini-14 .223 rifle. *(Courtesy Alaska State Troopers)*

Sherry Morrow. *(Courtesy Alaska State Troopers)*

"Eklutna Annie." Police artist's reconstruction based on decomposed remains.

Paula Goulding. *(Courtesy Alaska State Troopers)*

Abandoned today, the Wild Cherry bar on Fourth Avenue was part of Robert Hansen's hunting ground in Anchorage's "tenderloin" district. *(Bernard Du Clos)*

The Great Alaskan Bush Company, another topless club where Hansen stalked his victims. *(Bernard Du Clos)*

Sue Luna. *(Courtesy Alaska State Troopers)*

Tamara Pederson. *(Courtesy Alaska State Troopers)*

Andrea ("Fish") Altiery. *(Courtesy Alaska State Troopers)*

Joanne Messina. *(Courtesy Alaska State Troopers)*

The Sleeping Lady in Anchorage, a converted motel used by
the Seattle mob as a dormitory for its topless dancers.
(Bernard Du Clos)

Malai Larsen. *(Courtesy
Alaska State Troopers)*

Roxanne Easlund. *(Courtesy
Alaska State Troopers)*

Lisa Futrell. *(Courtesy Alaska
State Troopers)*

Angela Feddern. *(Courtesy
Alaska State Troopers)*

Robert Hansen's den, laden with his hunting trophies that included a world-record Dall sheep. Women came into his trophy room, some by polite invitation when they responded to his singles ad; others he brought at gunpoint.
(Courtesy Alaska State Troopers)

The custom-made fish necklace, found along with a cache of weapons in Hansen's attic, was a key piece of evidence linking Hansen to Andrea Altiery's disappearance.
(Courtesy Alaska State Troopers)

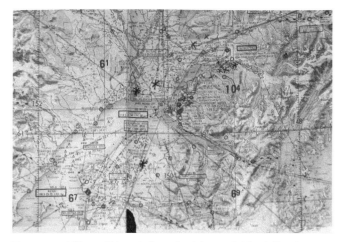

Hansen put Xs on this aviation chart to mark his victims' graves, which were scattered around Anchorage in the Mat-su Valley, and on the Kenai Peninsula. *(Bernard Du Clos)*

Sergeant Glenn Flothe *(left)* examines an unearthed corpse. *(Bernard Du Clos)*

In the spring of 1984, Alaska State Troopers discovered a body in the Knik River area. *(Bernard Du Clos)*

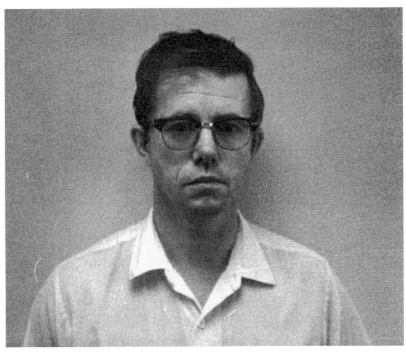

Portrait of a killer: Robert Hansen at his arraignment in
October 1983. *(Bernard Du Clos)*

and finally the reverend asked, "Could you ask me that question in another way?"

Gilmore complied. "Did anything you saw or hear this morning change your basic opinion in regard to the peacefulness of the conduct of Mr. Hansen?"

"No," was the pastor's abrupt reply.

Abrahamson went on to testify he'd known the Hansens four years, that they attended services and church functions on a regular basis, and that no, he wouldn't feel threatened if Robert were released.

Justin Ripley cross-examined. "This morning, you heard the witness, under oath, state that Robert Hansen is the man who raped her . . . ?"

"That's right," the reverend replied.

"Well," the prosecutor continued, "I take it that there is a credibility problem as to you finding that witness believable?"

"That's correct."

The prosecutor didn't put the witness on the spot and ask him why he didn't believe Barbara Fields. The reverend continued to maintain he felt very strongly that Hansen was innocent.

Barbara Fields watched as the minister stepped down and the second witness, Gerald Goldschmidt, took the stand. Goldschmidt, an environmental health officer for the Alaskan Native Health Service, testified he'd known Hansen since the fall of '68, hunted with him, that they were close friends and went to each other's homes. He couldn't believe that Bob would harm anyone, thought the state's witness must be mistaken, and felt Hansen should be released.

The third defense witness was John Sumrall, district manager for the Equitable Life Insurance Company, who hadn't been present at the morning session. He testified he'd known Hansen for three years, mostly as a hunting partner, and that he'd been with him when he bagged a world-record Dall sheep. He thought Robert would be no danger to the community if he were released.

The defense finished, and Fields took the stand and once again testified to her ordeal of December 19. Her voice was soft and lacking the confident tone of her testimony in the forenoon. She was feeling very much alone, hopelessly frustrated.

After she stepped down, final arguments were presented. Ripley stressed that Hansen's skills as a woodsman made him capable of disappearing into the Alaskan wilderness and surviving off the land.

The court continued Hansen's bail at $50,000, and he remained in custody.

On January 26 Hansen was indicted by a grand jury on three counts: kidnapping, rape, and assault with a deadly weapon. A week later he pleaded not guilty to all the charges, but continued to remain in custody.

In the Heppeard case, Dr. Langdon's psychiatric report found Hansen competent to stand trial, so proceedings resumed before Superior Court judge James M. Fitzgerald on March 2. The defense entered a plea of not guilty, and Gilmore put the state on notice of a possible psychiatric defense.

The Barbara Fields case was discussed at the hearing, and Judge Fitzgerald suggested having one case follow the other, setting the trial for both cases for the week of April 24.

Robert Hansen remained incarcerated at the South Central Regional Correctional Facility in Anchorage.

Until 1975, plea bargaining was an integral part of Alaska's adjudication of felonies, and it came into play in the Heppeard and Fields cases. By the time a change of plea hearing was held on March 22, 1972, all charges in the Fields case were dismissed.

In 1984 *Anchorage Daily News* reporter Sheila Toomey asked Justin Ripley, the prosecutor in the cases, why the charges in the Fields case were thrown out. Ripley, who had since become a judge, reviewed work records to refresh his memory and said, "The witness went down the drain." In her March 24 article, Toomey reported Ripley as saying the state offered to drop the weapon and kidnapping charges and recommend an eight-year sentence, with two suspended, if Hansen would plead guilty to the rape charges. The offer was refused twice, apparently because the defense was aware the state was having a witness problem.

Barbara Fields recalled: "No one thought I could continue with pressing charges . . . I guess I was coming apart.

"But it was like you're not only raped by the perpetrator, but again by the courts. . . ."

Barbara's experience with the system left her with a bitter memory she wouldn't forget.

A deal was finally made, however, and at the change-of-plea hearing, Hansen pleaded guilty in the Heppeard case. In turn, the prosecution recommended an eight-year sentence, with five suspended, and all the charges in the Fields case were dropped.

At the March 22 hearing, the defense called Dr. Ray Langdon to the stand, who testified that he'd diagnosed Hansen to suffer from schizophrenia. His conclusion was based on his interviews with the defendant and the psychiatric workups done on Hansen in Iowa in the early sixties.

Langdon said Hansen would suffer periods of disassociation during which he'd commit violent acts and not remember them. He felt Hansen's condition was treatable, and recommended twice-a-week psychiatric counseling for two to three years, and close supervision.

Hansen's strategy to pretend he "couldn't remember" had worked. His subsequent psychiatric treatment, based on this incorrect diagnosis, would be a farce.

John Sumrall and Gerald Goldschmidt once again vouched for Hansen's character, and said they thought their friend should be provided with psychiatric help and be allowed to return to his family and community.

In summary, the prosecution asked the defendant be given a three- or four-year sentence with parole and a treatment program lasting a minimum of two years. Gilmore pushed for a shorter sentence, reminding the court of Hansen's eight-year marriage, his infant daughter, and that he held two jobs to support his family.

Hansen stood before the bench for the court's decision.

Judge Fitzgerald said he was impressed by the persons who'd come forth as character witnesses for the defendant. "But, Mr. Hansen, I believe you have a serious illness that makes you extremely dangerous . . . one that requires therapy.

"I'm going to sentence you to five years in prison . . . eligible for parole if a psychiatrist can assure you're no longer a danger to the community.

"I recommend work release for you as soon as possible, so you can pursue your employment and support your family."

Robert Hansen had fooled the psychiatrist and played the system to his advantage, and it wouldn't be the last time. He continued to be jailed at the South Central Regional Correctional Facility, where he was a model prisoner. In less than three months he was transferred to a halfway house where he was on work release and received psychiatric treatment.

Over twelve years later, Hansen gave a chilling description of what was really going on in his mind at this point:

> While I was at the halfway house, at first my wife or an officer would drive me back and forth to work. Then, before long, I could drive myself.
>
> I'd drive downtown in a hurry and sit there and watch the prostitutes walking up and down the street, and I'd get a tremendous, gosh dang! I was parking there just to watch the prostitutes walking Fourth Avenue, because it give me this here sexual blowup charge.
>
> I got to thinking, right at that time, even when I was in jail, that boy, I couldn't wait till I could do it again!

Chapter 24

For six months Robert Hansen was a model resident at the halfway house, a good employee at the Safeway bakery, and a "cooperative" client at the Langdon Psychiatric Clinic.

At the end of November 1972, psychologist Dr. Allen H. Parker informed the parole board of Hansen's excellent progress in therapy, and how well he was handling his frequent work release and the weekend passes to visit his family. Parker concluded his report to the board: "Because of Hansen's demonstrated capacity to handle the freedom he now has, I recommend he be paroled."

Robert wasn't paroled, but he was released from the halfway house on "general furlough," which for all practical purposes was the same thing. His life was getting back to "normal."

The people who worked alongside Robert Hansen at the Safeway on Gambell Street had seen articles in the paper and heard talk about the charges against him —that he'd tied girls to the bed, one of them a policeman's daughter. But co-worker Irma Knight recalled, "We took it with a grain of salt, because Bob was a hard worker, the best cake decorator, and he had that little girl, so we figured he had a good marriage."

Hansen continued to use his family to create a facade of respectability to fool law enforcement professionals and persons in general—a tactic characteristic of the "organized" serial killer.

Barbara Fields had heard about Hansen's release a couple of weeks earlier. Driving home through the snow one night, she was sure she was being followed, *and sure it was Robert Hansen.*

Terrified, she kept going when she reached her parents' home; she was afraid her family might get hurt if something happened. Barbara drove past the house wondering if Hansen still had the address.

After a few blocks, she turned down a dead-end street, and the other car followed. With a tinge of satisfaction in her voice, she recalled how she got out of that tight spot:

"Now I was really good at doing 'brodies' . . . you know, on ice and snow you spin the car in a complete circle, or a half-brody, when you whip the rear of the car around and you're aimed the other way. Well, at the end of the street I did a half-brody, got out of there fast, and left the other car behind."

Barbara didn't tell her family about the incident. It's not uncommon for rape victims to conceal their fears and isolate themselves from the support of loved ones. That can be a significant hindrance to the recovery process.

Though Hansen appeared to be on good behavior during his general furlough, two asterisks along Resurrection Bay at Seward found on the aviation map he used to mark the graves of his victims indicated otherwise.

Located 128 miles south of Anchorage on the Kenai Peninsula, Seward is a small town nestled between Mount Marathon and Resurrection Bay. Besides a fish cannery, a state vocational school, a resort, and a shipbuilding and repair industry, it has a small boat harbor where Robert Hansen moored his thirty-six-foot Chris-Craft, the *Christy M,* in the seventies.

The boat slept six, and Robert used it for a lot of fishing and hunting activities. Gloria didn't go on the boat much because she got seasick easily, but the couple did fish for halibut off Chevelle Island and drop bottom nets for pink shrimp and crab near Driftwood Cove. Hansen liked to anchor in Thumbs Cove and hunt black bear and goats on shore and the nearby hills, where an abundance of skunk cabbage lured game into the area.

Once, some divers chartered Hansen's boat to explore the bay to see if there were enough sea cucumbers to make commercial harvesting feasible. There weren't, but Hansen made out well. He not only got the fee for the charter, the men also taught him how to scuba dive. Hansen liked to dive around the rock piles off the "Iron Doors," where there were lots of fish, and pods of sea lions and whales in the spring.

It's speculated that the first mark at Resurrection Bay went on Hansen's map in 1973. His wife hadn't seen her folks for a couple of years, and her parents had never seen their new granddaughter. So mother and daughter flew down to the lower forty-eight to spend part of the summer of '73 with Gloria's folks, leaving Robert Hansen behind in Alaska, all by himself.

On July 7, 1973, seventeen-year-old Megan Emerick took her washing to the laundromat in the Seward Skills Center girl's dormitory. When her clothes were dried, she carried them back to her room. After hanging, folding, and putting them away, she decided to go into town.

The five-foot-three Megan stood in front of her mirror and ran a brush through her long blond hair, which was complemented by big, hazel eyes. She left the dorm—and disappeared without a trace.

Irma Knight, Hansen's coworker at Safeway, went into the wilderness with him, and lived to tell about it. She went hunting with Robert in the fall of '73.

"Bob had wanted us to come over to his house to see his trophies," Irma said, "but we never went . . . it wasn't that kind of friendship. But as a favor, he was my guide for a goat hunt."

Mr. and Mrs. Knight sailed their Chris-Craft down to Seward, and while Mr. Knight stayed on their boat in a cove, Irma went up the mountain with Hansen.

She remembered that Robert was very nice and considerate during the hunt:

"We stopped for lunch, an apple and a candy bar. He was sitting above me on the slope, and he said, 'Now don't be scared, but look up.' I did, and saw two porcupines above me in the tree I was resting against.

"We worked our way above the goats, and I shot mine with a rifle. It didn't look big enough to be a trophy, but Bob said to shoot it anyway. It fell off the cliff, and retrieving the carcass was sort of scary because we were in a slide area. But everything turned out okay."

The Knights bought the Sportsman's Inn in Whittier that winter, and the next summer both of them hunted with Hansen down at Seward. A fall sheep hunt they planned with him didn't materialize, and they never hunted with him after that.

Hansen did have an encounter with Seward police, however. They found a stolen boat motor and a depth finder, with the serial numbers filed off, aboard the *Christy M.* Hansen contended he'd bought them through private sales but had lost the receipts. He passed a lie detector test and wasn't charged.

Consequently, with no record of bad behavior or misconduct during his general furlough, he was paroled in December of '73.

Hansen raped a sixteen-year-old girl in Anchorage in 1974, but it wasn't reported. Ten years after the assault, the victim told her story to Sheila Toomey, who was writing a series of articles about "the hidden victims of violent crimes" in the *Anchorage Daily News.* In the June 12, 1984, story the victim was given the pseudonym "Leila."

Under a panorama of northern lights on a brisk September night, Leila was walking home to Gambell Street after a party. The open fronts of her party shoes were letting her toes get cold.

As she crossed a street, a man waiting in a parked car rolled down his window and asked if she wanted a ride. Though she didn't usually hitchhike, the man was soft-spoken and polite—he didn't seem threatening. She accepted.

"He sort of looked like the perfect dork," Leila told Toomey. "I thought he was a dud."

At her house, Robert Hansen wouldn't let her out of the car, and pulled a gun when she tried to resist. Terror gripped the young woman as they drove away.

Leila remembered Hansen getting very talkative, asking about her boyfriend: Did she sleep with him? How many boys had she slept with?

"I had a gun to my head, so I thought honesty was the best policy and answered his questions. I had the feeling he had done this kind of thing before."

Hansen made her take off everything except her blouse, and then he forced her to perform oral sex on him while he held the gun to her head. After that, he made her flash a passing motorist. This forced "public" humiliation of the flashing illustrated his need to dominate his victim.

After several hours of making Leila please him, Hansen drove around trying to find, as he put it—"another girl to make us do things." He didn't find anyone.

"Then he drove around aimlessly for a long while," Leila said. "I thought he was trying to decide what to do with me."

Suddenly, Robert Hansen handed her the gun and said, "Okay, now you can do whatever you want with me, or you can order me to drive you to the police station."

It's hard to tell what he may have had in mind at this point. That he felt guilty and wanted to be arrested is very doubtful. Serial rapist-killers are seldom, if ever, remorseful; Robert Hansen has never expressed remorse. An urge for self-destruction is not uncommon among criminals like Hansen; he could have wanted her to shoot him. But most likely, it was the control game that Leila suspected; her captor was toying with her.

"I had the gun in my hand," Leila told Toomey. "I could have shot the bastard. But I thought it was a trap, that the gun wasn't even loaded."

The man finally let her go, threatening, "If you go to the police, I'll hunt you down."

The terrified Leila responded, "Just let me live, I'll never tell."

She kept her promise and never went to the police. Leila did tell her foster parents, who were waiting up for her, that she had been raped. They offered to call the police for her, but she declined.

The next day, the victim of violence became the victim of blame. Leila's foster parents called social service authorities and asked that she be taken out of their home. They didn't give a reason.

While on probation, Hansen reported to his parole officer in a government building that housed other social service agencies.

In the fall of 1974 Barbara Fields was in that building completing the papers to assume official custody of her child. She was happy that she was now in a position to take responsibility for her son.

Finished with the forms and procedure, she headed for the elevator, where her elation plunged to fear. Getting into the elevator, Barbara pivoted and faced Robert Hansen, about to walk on.

Hansen recognized her, too. He hesitated, then withdrew.

"Thank God he didn't get on!" Barbara said. "He saw I was scared to death!"

Trembling, Fields ran out of the building to her brand new red and white Plymouth Duster, scrambled into the security of its all-white interior and sped off.

"I drove like a maniac," she recalled. "I was so upset I almost ran a red light and wrecked my new car."

Barbara never told her family about that incident either.

. . .

It's believed that the second asterisk along Resurrection Bay was drawn on Robert Hansen's aviation chart in 1975.

Mary K. Thill was twenty-three years old, five-foot-five, had long and wavy red hair, and wore thick, round glasses in pink frames. She was dressed in Levi's, a gray pullover sweater, hiking boots, and had a small backpack with her when some friends gave her a ride from her Lowell Point home into Seward on July 5. After they dropped her off, she disappeared.

Thill's husband was away from home, working up at Prudhoe in the new oil field on the North Slope. Finding out his wife was missing, he returned home and put up a $1,000 reward for any information as to Mary's whereabouts or disappearance. It went unclaimed.

Later in the summer of '75, Hansen visited his parents at their new home in Pendleton, Oregon.

Returning to Anchorage, Hansen's violent escapades with women continued. He went bar hopping one October night in 1975: "I stopped at the clubs and went in and watched the girls take off their clothes and dance in front of me.

"I gave them five dollars for a table dance, and they would come up and shake their tits, or put their tits in front of my nose. . . ."

At the Kit Kat Club on Old Seward Highway, Hansen approached a dancer about "having some fun later on." He flashed a roll of money and said he'd just arrived in Alaska to work on the new oil pipeline. She agreed to meet him after her shift.

Later, in the parking lot of a restaurant called the Fork and Spoon at the corner of Old Seward and Tudor Drive, the dancer got into Hansen's car.

Robert Hansen's own words provide a vivid and frightening portrayal of how viciously calculating and practiced the modus operandi of a violent serial criminal generally is:

I tried to act as tough as I could, right away, so as to get them as scared as possible and get control. Even before I started talking, I would reach over, get my hand in the girl's hair, and then jerk her head back and put a gun in her face . . . get 'em to feel helpless, scared . . .

After he got control that night, he took the woman to the foothills in Chugach State Park, raped her, then let her go.

The victim went to a rape crisis center and made a positive identification of her assailant from a photo file. She remembered the license number of his vehicle, and identified the firearm Hansen put to her head as a Model 38 Smith & Wesson.

But the woman refused to go to police headquarters and file charges. A schoolteacher up in Alaska to earn some big money, she didn't want any publicity. In terror of her assailant, she fled the state the next day.

State Trooper Sam Barnard took the investigation as far as he could without formal charges being filed by the victim. The license number she'd given checked out to Robert Hansen, and Barnard became convinced he was guilty. He told Hansen's parole officer, Wayne Burgess, what he suspected.

When Burgess confronted Hansen about the incident, Hansen admitted being with the woman, but with a stutter said, "I thought it was a date . . . then she asked for money, and I refused to pay. So, she gets mad and hollers rape."

This wouldn't be the last time Hansen used this ruse with authorities. The parole officer didn't believe it, but unfortunately there was nothing he could do about it.

Chapter 25

When Robert Hansen was paroled in 1973, Alaska and Anchorage were bracing for the biggest boom since the Alaskan Gold Rush. The House of Representatives, and then the U.S. Senate, had just passed a conference bill that permitted the construction of a trans-Alaskan pipeline. The November 13 vote in the upper legislative body had capped five years of business maneuvering and political theatre—a saga of control over men and earth played on a grand scale by powerful factions. Indirectly, it would play a significant role in the drama of Robert Hansen's lust to control women.

In 1968 a large oil deposit was discovered on the North Slope of Alaska. Eleven years earlier an oil find on the Kenai Peninsula had been successfully exploited because the Kenai fields were adjacent to ice-free ports. However, to tap the deposit of black gold on the North Slope, there would have to be a way to get the crude oil out of the frozen north to tankers waiting in an ice-free harbor; ergo, a pipeline through Alaska's tundra, permafrost, and wilderness.

At the same time that a proposal for an 800-mile, $1 billion pipeline from Prudhoe Bay to Valdez was crystallizing, so was the Environmental Protection Act of 1969, which could block its construction.

Enter the Nixon administration. Its Department of Interior hastily leased out huge coal-rich tracts of land in western states to the large oil and mining companies. Paying just pennies an acre—a rate established in 1872 by the Mining Act—the companies sat on the coal deposits, rendering them unavailable. And, despite advice to the contrary from career professionals within the Department of Interior, an oil-import quota program was vigorously maintained, which effectively applied a tourniquet to the flow of foreign oil into the United States.

By the time Richard Nixon fired his Secretary of the Interior, Walter Hickel, on Thanksgiving eve, 1970, Americans faced the threat of an empty oil barrel as they were told an energy shortage was developing that could put their country into crisis.

In January 1971 the Interior Department released a 195-page feasibility study of a trans-Alaskan pipeline. Unavoidable environmental damage would have to be necessary, the report concluded, "because the oil rich fields of the Arctic North Slope are essential to the strength, growth, and security of the United States."

Three months later, in April, a coalition of conservation groups secured a court injunction prohibiting the Department of Interior from issuing licenses or permits for the construction of an Alaskan pipeline. A battle was on.

But the oil companies, the Nixon administration, and eventually Congress, pushed for the pipeline project. They won the war two years later, when the U.S. Supreme Court, with a limp-wristed backhand of jurisprudence, declined to review the lower court injunction blocking the pipeline permits. That lobbed the ball to Congress' court, where the legislation necessary for the project to move ahead soon passed.

Pipeline construction began in early '74 under the banner of the Alyeska Pipeline Service Company, a consortium of seven oil companies. What looked to be a $1 billion endeavor in 1969 was now projected to be $5 billion; the final cost would be $7.7 billion.

Suddenly, Alaska had more than 30,000 laborers earning a thousand dollars a week working on the pipeline. Ten thousand of them poured in from out of state, and overnight Alaska's population increased by three percent.

As there'd been business entrepreneurs, tradesmen, and service persons coming with prospectors during the Gold Rush, now they came to do business, serve, and/or exploit this gusher of prosperity. All of this population increase was ensconced in Anchorage and towns on or near the pipeline route between Prudhoe Bay and Valdez.

As inflation had hit the cost of the pipeline, it now slammed into Alaska. Housing and general living costs soared. A $20,000 house in Anchorage sold for $52,000, rents tripled, and the price of a plain steak dinner went to twenty dollars. For those who were part of the pipeline construction or in a position to dip into its resultant cash flow, it was a boon, but for the many out of that mainstream, it meant enduring the inflation and putting up with other undesirable developments, including a soaring crime rate.

In Fairbanks, the number of prostitutes on the 500 block of Second Street quadrupled, as did their prices. Longtime Alaska residents adopted new practices, like locking their homes and autos. A strain was put on community utilities and services, and there were "outsiders" living in their vehicles because they couldn't find housing or, because when they arrived in Alaska full of expectations of finding work, they found all the jobs were filled. Tensions built, and outsiders from Texas and Oklahoma were sneeringly called "pointed shoes" because of their cowboy boots. Bumper stickers appeared that read ALYESKA GO HOME.

In the midst of the pain and prosperity, pipeline construction proceeded at breakneck speed. In 1990, on the heels of the Exxon Valdez oil spill disaster, the *Los Angeles Times* would report corrosion threatened the pipeline, and numerous violations committed during its hurried construction were the cause.

Historically, Seattle businessmen played a significant if not always benevolent role in Alaska's economy. Now the stories coming out of Alaska about big bankrolls and a rough and tumble open frontier atmosphere caught the attention of Seattle's organized crime. The Colacurcio organization—run by Frank Colacurcio—operated a string of topless bars and pornography and gambling rings in Seattle and several Pacific Northwest and Gulf states. Frank, convicted in 1972 for conspiracy in the interstate transportation of gambling devices, and for violations of federal racketeering laws, was serving time at Washington's McNeil Island penitentiary when the pipeline construction started.

From his cell at McNeil, which he shared with Gilbert "Junior" Pauole in the mid-seventies, Frank Colacurcio masterminded his organization's move to the north. Alaska's liquor licensing laws provided the ideal situation because they allowed a corporate name to go on a liquor license, permitting the corporation or its listed officers to front for a crime organization or convicted felons who controlled an operation.

In 1975 Colacurcio associates purchased a liquor license behind the corporate name Goldies Inc. and leased a building at 122 East Fourth Avenue in Anchorage. They opened a topless-bottomless bar called the Booby Trap. Stanford Poll was installed as the club's manager.

Across the street, at 145 East Fourth, Poll managed another club. The building was rented from Neil Mackay, well-known lawyer and real estate mogul, who'd once used it as a morgue for his undertaking business. The club would have different names but would be remembered most as the Wild Cherry.

At the Wild Cherry, Poll was in partnership with Howard Swerland, the brother-in-law of Norman Adams. Adams ran pornography stores in Washington State. The Wild Cherry's liquor license was listed under the corporate name Swerland Inc.

Colacurcio's henchmen established an alliance with the Anchorage Brothers motorcycle gang, hiring its members to work in the clubs and to do "enforcing or urging errands." The Seattle mob was heeding a lesson learned the hard way by organized crime in Chicago. In the early seventies a Chicago motorcycle gang bombed a dozen of the Mafia's massage parlors when the mob refused to hire the cyclists' girls at inflated wages. Giving the Brothers a little action up front, Colacurcio's henchmen reasoned, could probably save some headaches down the line.

The Talents West agency, operated by the Colacurcio organization in Seattle, provided the Booby Trap and Wild Cherry with topless dancers. As Colacurcio's empire expanded to other Anchorage and Kodiak Island bars, those and other independent clubs "urged to do so" would feature entertainment supplied by Talents West. The agency shipped dancers to several states besides Alaska— Texas, Louisiana, California, Hawaii, and, as Frank Colacurcio put it, "throughout the West."

Talents West's recurring ad in the *Seattle Post Intelligencer* read:

$$$ BIG MONEY $$$
DANCERS surrounding Seattle & Alaska areas.
Full & part time / no fee.
No exp. required. Call Mon.-Sat.
from 11–7. ###-####.

Women who responded to the ad hoping for big money found a bondage of indenture instead. A call to the number in the ad led to a quickly arranged interview at the Talents West office on Lake City Way, near the Sea-Tac Airport. At the sparsely furnished office they had a brief interview—after his release from McNeil in July 1976, it would be with Frank "Papa" Colacurcio—and were immediately offered a job without dancing a single step. The women were promised big money and fringes if they'd work in Alaska—$500 a day, generous tips, airfare, and a place to live.

It could all sound wonderful to a young woman in search of a good income, but the promises fizzled when the dancers arrived in Alaska. Their housing in downtown Anchorage was crowded and dingy, and the clubs were drab and full of rowdy, surly customers.

The first payday punctuated the writing on the wall. Typical deductions from their first week's check were: airfare—$200, rent—$75, costume—$75, and a three-dollar kickback to the house for every hour worked. The bottom line of the first week was a minus—a dancer "owed the company." And there was no ticket home if she wanted to quit.

A former dancer summed up the situation this way:

> What you had was a very scared, transient girl whose only friends were other dancers and the creeps that came in the bars. She didn't have anybody to turn to . . . she was confused, in a game that was over her head. . . .

Many of those dancers would sink deeper—into drugs, in with a pimp, or both. Some would escape from Alaska by securing help from a private social service organization. Others would try to make a quick chunk of cash to buy a plane ticket, like accepting an offer of $300 from a man who stuttered and had a pockmarked face.

Chapter 26

The pipeline economy expanded business for Anchorage wholesalers. In 1975, as a Teamster, Robert Hansen took a second job as a laborer on the loading dock at Alaska Cold Storage. The Hansens now had a baby son, and with two children, they were saving to buy a larger home.

By July 1976 Robert and Gloria were able to put a $37,000 downpayment on an $88,000 house on Old Harbor Avenue in Muldoon. Hansen's parents came to visit in September and see their son's new home.

But being a person of means didn't stop Robert Hansen's thievery, one reason being his pathological frugality—he "just hated to pay for things." But mainly it was for the thrill of it all. When he shoplifted, he'd come close to ejaculating in his pants—it gave him the same satisfaction he got with a prostitute.

In the bicentennial year's presidential election the day before, American voters had elected the first President to come from the Deep South in 125 years. At the Fred Meyer Store at the intersection of Northern Lights Boulevard and the New Seward Highway, the post-election day shopping crowd was sparse.

Security guard Jessie G. Smith watched a shopper act suspiciously in the sporting goods section. At the chain-saw display, the man's pockmarked face turned one way, then the other, as he examined a saw. It appeared to Smith that the fellow was looking to see if anyone was watching him.

Abruptly, the man left the store.

A few minutes later Smith saw him again, heading for the chain saws. Following him, the guard watched the man pick a sales slip off the floor and stick it on the box of a $179 McCullough chain saw, then take the box through a closed checkout lane and out of the store.

Smith pursued, and apprehended Robert Hansen eighty yards from the entrance. The sales receipt stuck on the box was for eleven dollars.

A week later Hansen was indicted by a grand jury for a felony—larceny in a building. The District Attorney could have prosecuted the offense as a shoplifting misdemeanor, but sought a felony charge because of Hansen's previous convictions. At his arraignment, Hansen pleaded not guilty and was released on $500 bail.

Hansen took immediate steps to prepare for a psychological defense: He went back to see psychologist Dr. Allen Parker.

After administering a series of tests, Parker wrote an evaluation that contrasted sharply with the recommendation he'd given to Hansen's parole board four years earlier:

> Emotional and personality testing indicate a markedly disturbed man . . . somewhat antisocial, paranoid by nature, and with a relatively weak ego.
>
> There are indications of severe heterosexual conflict, both with a desire for women and a fear that he will not be able to relate to them. He is capable of acting out impulses, and he's aware of many of the impulses within his personality. He has a great deal of free floating anxiety.

Parker had the records of Hansen's tests from 1972, so he was able to do a longitudinal analysis:

> The retesting indicates the presence of disintegration of personality to a highly potential psychotic level or high schizophrenic scale, high manic scale, and high antisocial scale . . . there's some narcissism and magical thinking involved in this also.

This ominous evaluation wasn't the kind of expert witness testimony a defense likes to pay for. Hansen proceeded to see psychiatrist Dr. Barth McManmon at the Alaska Clinic.

With the strength of the prosecution's evidence, the defense cut to the chase with a change-of-plea hearing on January 19, 1977, where before Judge James K. Singleton, Hansen pleaded guilty to the theft of the chain saw and spun an obviously contrived tale as to why he did it.

He said he'd wanted to give the saw to his father as a Christmas present—to please him. But since he and his wife had invested all their savings in their new house in Muldoon, he was strapped for cash. But he *sure* wanted to give that chain saw to his dad, who was sixty-nine years old, overweight, and had already suffered one heart attack.

Hansen said that when he'd left the store without the saw, he ran into the scene of a man having a heart attack in the Fred Meyer parking lot. That made him decide to go back in the store and steal the saw to give to his father. "I know what I did was wrong and I'm very sorry for doing so."

Ronald Offret, Hansen's attorney, requested a delay of at least six weeks to allow preparation of a psychiatric report by Dr. McManmon, who was now treating Hansen. The judge granted the request, and the defendant would continue to be free on $500 bail until proceedings resumed on March 22.

During his release in February, Hansen tried to get a pilot's license, indicating on his application he was taking lithium. Denied a license because of the drug, he quickly reapplied, this time listing no drug use. But the examiner checked the file of rejected applications and caught him in his lie. Hansen would never have a pilot's license.

On March 22 Dr. McManmon testified he'd diagnosed Hansen as suffering from a bipolar effective disorder, a variant of a manic depressive disorder. The doctor distinguished Robert's affliction from the classic manic-depressive pattern by the absence of any serious depressive episodes. Hansen's impulses, he said, were poorly controlled during his mood and energy upswings, in which he developed an abnormal preoccupation with a single activity. His kleptomania was a manifestation of this monomania, and his determination as a trophy hunter was a socially acceptable example of his monomanic behavior, "where he'd be looking to do things no one else had done to consume his energy."

McManmon said that after his third session with Hansen, it was evident to him that Robert's antisocial urges were escalating, so he prescribed Thorazine to put an immediate check on those impulses. McManmon described Thorazine as a tranquilizer.

The Thorazine stabilized Hansen, McManmon said, but it interfered with his ability to function normally at work. After conferring with Dr. Parker, he'd switched his patient to lithium, which McManmon described as "a prophylactic that shortened the amplitude and duration of Hansen's manic swings," allowing him to function normally while learning how to control his antisocial behavior.

Prosecutor James Gould asked McManmon how long it would take the defendant to learn to control himself. The doctor wouldn't assure Hansen's future behavior, but he said with the lithium, Hansen had developed a good rapport toward treatment, and he didn't anticipate any problems if the therapy continued. While it was possible that Hansen would have to remain on lithium indefinitely, McManmon believed the prognosis to be favorable.

The case was continued to April 5, Hansen to remain free on bail.

At the proceedings two weeks later, parole officer Wayne Burgess's testimony before Judge Singleton delved into Robert Hansen's history of aberrant, violent sexual behavior, talking at length about Hansen's alleged rape of the dancer from the Kit Kat Club in 1975.

Burgess testified that the State Trooper who had investigated the allegation was convinced of Hansen's guilt. The parole officer said that he himself talked to the victim while she was at the rape crisis center, and he felt she told the truth but was too terrified of Hansen to press charges. "I was concerned because this allegation typified a hundred percent Hansen's original offense in 1971."

Burgess said that on several occasions he'd found Robert downtown prowling the bars late at night, and had repeatedly urged him to return to counseling, particularly after the Kit Kat Club incident. "But Bob refused . . . he said he didn't need counseling."

The parole officer felt strongly that Hansen should be locked up. And contrary to what Dr. McManmon testified, Burgess doubted that Hansen would cooperate and respond to therapy now.

Arguments concluded, Judge Singleton discussed the sentence he was about to impose, unaware of the ironies in his words.

First of all, he said that he found it to be a difficult case. Singleton stated that he would not take Parole Officer Burgess's testimony into consideration because the Kit Kat Club allegation and his subsequent observations had never been verified by the legal process.

The two goals of the sentence he would pronounce, the judge said, would be for the rehabilitation of the defendant, and the protection of the community:

> . . . Dr. McManmon has testified Mr. Hansen has a psychiatric disability that requires counseling and doses of lithium . . . I've given serious consideration to putting Mr. Hansen on some kind of methadone program, substituting lithium for the methadone and requiring reporting to the Division of Corrections . . .
>
> Mr. Hansen is dangerous. I think Dr. McManmon made clear that during the manic phase of his condition, he is capable of committing crimes. His behavior, whatever his capacity to control it, is largely uncontrolled.
>
> . . . To suspend imposition of sentence or to provide straight probation would not be appropriate in light of the fact that Mr. Hansen has been on probation in the past and apparently the supervision wasn't sufficient to prevent him from criminal activity.

Before passing sentence, Judge Singleton asked the defendant if he had anything to say.

Hansen responded with a carefully prepared statement wherein he used his family as a shield and cast himself as more a victim than a perpetrator.

He spoke controlled and politely, saying how his current treatment with Dr. McManmon had made him a new person. With the lithium doses, he no longer stuttered, and his former shame about his speech problem had been replaced with self-esteem.

Hansen reminded the court of his wife and two children, and said they would be made to suffer if he was imprisoned. He said he wanted to be out of jail so he could support them.

Claiming his thieving days were over, he said he now felt proud to walk out of a store knowing he paid for his merchandise with money he'd earned.

In conclusion, he asked the court to mandate that he get treatment, saying, "I want to live a life that's acceptable to society and to myself."

The judge complemented Hansen for speaking "eloquently" on his own behalf, then sentenced him to five years in prison.

Singleton ended his pronouncement of sentence:

> . . . during that time you should receive psychiatric treatment, and under no circumstances should you be admitted to parole without first having established for you a program of psychiatric counseling and therapy.

Interestingly, the judge then asked the District Attorney where Hansen would be sent by the Department of Corrections.

Prosecutor James Gould answered that with a five-year sentence, it would probably be the Juneau Correctional Institute.

Singleton voiced concern, because he knew there were no provisions for psychiatric rehabilitation treatment at that facility. "Juneau is simply a warehouse," he sighed.

Two days after his sentencing, Hansen's attorney filed a notice of appeal.

On April 21, when he was classified to serve his sentence at the correction center in Juneau, Hansen had his lawyer file a motion to have the sentence reduced. The defense's argument was that by reducing the sentence to three years, Hansen could be reclassified to the Eagle River correction facility, where he could receive psychiatric treatment.

At the ensuing hearing on August 16, Judge Singleton denied the motion, staying with the five-year sentence, reflecting that it was, after all, Hansen's third felony conviction. As to the issue of treatment, the judge said Hansen would be transferred to Eagle River after two years at Juneau, and his therapy and treatment could be reestablished then.

Regrettably, the scenario Singleton envisioned wouldn't come to pass.

Chapter 27

Hansen continued his appeal, filing a brief with the Alaska Supreme Court in October 1977. In its appellant's statement of facts, Hansen was depicted as a well-respected family man, hardworking, an owner of a home and three vehicles, a records-holding bow hunter, an active member of several sport organizations, and a steady attendant at the Abbott Loop Christian Center. Playing to the myth that sports automatically build character, his high athletic career was distorted: "Hansen was active in sports, particularly football and track, in which he held school records."

It was also noted that he was enrolled in a private pilot ground-school course just prior to his current imprisonment.

The appellant's argument to the court stated: "Mr. Hansen's first conviction for arson occurred at an age when many people are particularly susceptible to skirmishes with the law. The offense was against property, with no aggravating circumstances."

Actually, the arson had been an assault against people. And the brief distorted the reality of Hansen's second conviction, for assault with a deadly weapon. It stated the circumstances surrounding the 1971 assault of Susan Heppeard were unclear, "but there appeared to be no aggravating circumstances."

Obviously, Miss Heppeard had been more than aggravated by having a gun pointed at her head. And, unfortunately, since the plea bargaining in 1972 had erased the indictments for kidnap and rape against Hansen in the Barbara Fields case, the brief's appellant argument didn't have to deal with that at all.

The argument did go on to state that the chain-saw theft could have been charged as a misdemeanor, since the saw's value was less than the amount usually necessary for felony theft to be prosecuted, and that the appellant saw the gift of a chain saw as an opportunity to impress his father, who'd always been critical of him.

The ludicrous brief concluded that three felony convictions "hardly qualify Mr. Hansen as an habitual criminal," and requested he be released on probation under psychiatric care, or have his sentence reduced.

The Supreme Court of Alaska digested the "facts," and on August 11, 1978, filed its written opinion in the Hansen case:

. . . The record before us reveals a man suffering from a clearly diagnosed mental illness that until recently offered little hope of recovery . . . Hansen's psychiatrist prescribed a course of drug treatment and therapy, and reported to the sentencing court that Hansen had been cooperative and had a positive attitude toward the treatment . . .

Hansen's prior convictions were five and fifteen years, before the chain-saw offense. During that time, Hansen has otherwise conducted his life in a normal manner. He has maintained steady employment, been a good provider, and has earned the reputation of a hard worker and a respectable member of the community. It's quite possible that the convictions stemmed as much from psychological aberration as from a criminal propensity. Dr. McManmon testified that the chances of Hansen engaging in future criminal activity would be greatly reduced by lithium treatment and continued therapy.

The judges' opinion accepted the linkage of mental illness to Hansen's antisocial behavior. They expressed optimism about the treatment Dr. McManmon was giving his patient, and considering Hansen's stable home and work environment, their decision concluded that he be put on probation for the remainder of his five-year sentence. Also . . .

The terms of probation should be fixed by the Superior Court . . . to reflect the importance of Hansen's cooperation with his psychiatric treatment and to supervise the course of his progress. We remand with directions that the Superior Court place Hansen on parole as expeditiously as possible.

Chief Justice Robert Boochever and Justices Roger Connor, Jay Rabinowitz, and Warren Matthews concurred in the decision. Justice Edmund Burke dissented: "Given Hansen's record, I am unable to agree."

The stage was now set for yet one more blunder by the judiciary.

Judge Singleton ordered Robert Hansen's release on August 31, and a hearing to establish the conditions of his parole was held on September 14. Hansen didn't attend; it was hunting season, so he was probably out in the wilderness.

Singleton began the proceedings saying he assumed Hansen would be under the regular conditions of parole, and that it would probably be in his best interest to continue therapy and taking lithium.

In fact, Robert Hansen's lithium and psychiatric therapy had stopped completely when he was sent to Juneau, and he hadn't resumed it when he got back to the Anchorage area.

Assistant District Attorney James Gould interjected that he thought specific guidelines should be established to ensure Hansen would get the treatment he needed.

Judge Singleton disagreed:

I don't think so. The only way you'd learn he's not participating in treatment is if he committed another crime. To order Mr. Hansen to stay on any kind of medical program or medicine would probably be inappropriate . . . of course it's in his best interest to do it . . . When he's off, he's apparently at risk.

Singleton was not being consistent with what he'd said when he sentenced Hansen. At that time he stated in no uncertain terms that Hansen shouldn't be paroled without specific guidelines for psychiatric treatment.

Reminding the judge of Hansen's history of not following through with therapy programs, Gould continued to push for establishing guidelines and rules.

The Superior Court judge continued to resist:

Mr. Gould, for the record, I'm absolutely convinced that Mr. Hansen is going to commit additional crimes. I don't even think that's an open question. But in this case the Supreme Court has indicated that as long as the crimes are against property, not crimes of violence, the community is just going to have to tolerate it.

It's difficult to ascertain how, from the Supreme Court's written decision, Judge Singleton could have fathomed that the higher court was giving a green light to any offenses against property. Most likely, he was venting some frustration that *his* decision had been overturned by the other court.

Now, Prosecutor Gould went the last mile, and as tactfully as possible pointed out to the judge that the Supreme Court decision included a directive that specific guidelines for psychiatric treatment and drug regimen be established for Hansen's parole.

Singleton relented. After some discussion of the details of the treatment program with the prosecutor and Hansen's attorney, Ronald Offret, the judge directed Gould to prepare, for the court's signature, an order that would list the conditions of Hansen's parole to include a supervised lithium and therapy program. Then the hearing adjourned.

Almost two months later, November 6, 1978, Judge Singleton's secretary, Leah Hojem, sent a memo to Criminal Records:

Criminal,

James Gould in the DA's Office is supposed to submit an order setting out the conditions of probation [for Robert Hansen], but as of today he still has not done this. I put in a call to his office this morning and intend to remind him of the order. In the meantime, I'm sending this case back down to you, and when the order finally reaches your office go ahead and route the file and order back to me.

Thanks so much.
L.

Eight days later, Leah Hojem added a notation to her copy of the memo: "11-14-78 Sent copy of memo to remind Jim Gould."

And finally, almost three years later, another notation was added to the memo copy: "8-20-81 resent."

Court-ordered guidelines for Robert Hansen's parole were never issued. The Supreme Court's mandamus wasn't followed, and Hansen's release remained totally unsupervised.

Just a few weeks after his release from prison, Robert Hansen murdered a black woman at Summit Lake on the Kenai Peninsula. She was the first of at least seventeen women he would kill between that fall of 1978 and his arrest in 1983.

Chapter 28

In 1977, while Robert Hansen was in prison, his buddy John Sumrall enjoyed some good bow hunting. In August, as the first oil flowed through the pipeline from Prudhoe to Valdez and into a waiting tanker, Sumrall brought down a Rocky Mountain goat along the Fox River on the Kenai Peninsula that ranked fifty-fourth in Pope and Young. And just north of the Knik River, he shot a black bear that ranked 361st.

When Robert was released in '78, just in time for most of the hunting season, he and Sumrall resumed their camaraderie in the outdoors.

One of their favorite haunts was the Knik River north of Anchorage. Many times they walked its banks and sprawling sandbars, carrying blunts or sawed-off broad heads (arrows) to practice shooting their bows from different, undetermined ranges: "We'd be walking along, and I'd say, 'John, that tree stump up there is a world record!' And we'd shoot at it, say from twenty-five yards, or sometimes maybe fifty.

"We'd retrieve our arrows and maybe shoot a little stick lying nearby. It was much better practice for hunting than shooting a bale of hay at a determined distance."

The practice paid off for Sumrall; he bagged an Alaskan-Yukon moose in the Yenlo Mountains in '79 that ranked thirteenth in Pope and Young.

But Robert Hansen followed a new track, and bought a .223-caliber Ruger Mini-14, a semiautomatic weapon similar in appearance to the military M-16.

He said he bought the gun to shoot fox, coyotes, and wolves: "It was a weapon I could have two or three clips for. You know, when you jump on coyotes two or three at a time, especially in March when they're running and mating, you can get off a lot of shots quickly. It's quite accurate up to 150 yards."

Eventually the Mini-14 would become Hansen's weapon of choice for his two-legged victims.

Getting access to an airplane, Hansen began to fly to the Knik River area to practice to become a crack bush pilot.

On the river's big, flat sandbars there was no air traffic to contend with, so, as Hansen put it, he "could go and go and go." Laying pine trees at each end of his wilderness runway, he'd land between them, then keep moving the pines closer and closer together to practice shorter landings.

Robert Hansen's monomania gave him a tenacity to focus and develop skills he'd put to deadly use. Though it was never verified that he shot any of his female victims while they were on the ground and he was flying in his airplane, he did shoot wolves from a plane with his .223 Mini-14. Again, the Knik River area was the place he practiced to hone that skill.

He'd throw balloons weighted with a nut or sinker into the river's slow-moving current. Then, going up in his airplane, he'd shoot at them, and the splashes in the water told him where his bullets were hitting. In the winter, instead of balloons, he'd shoot at ice chunks floating down the river.

But the hunting and stalking that was Robert Hansen's obsession didn't take place in the wilderness or in the air, but on the streets and in the bars of downtown Anchorage, where, it seemed, society and its judicial system were giving him the license to "go and go and go."

On October 14, 1979, Christie Hayes was dancing at the Embers, a club in downtown Anchorage. She did a table dance for a fellow who was sitting by himself, nursing a beer. The man's gaze trailed up her black legs, and through his glasses his eyes met hers. He flashed a roll of money, and with a stutter asked if they could meet later.

"I'll be off in twenty minutes," she told him.

"Good. We'll meet outside . . . look for a gold camper."

Later, after Hayes got into the back of the camper on an agreement to perform oral sex, Hansen pulled a gun. But this time there was a glitch in his routine when he grabbed his victim by the hair—Christie was wearing a wig, and it came off when he gave it a yank.

But he quickly recovered and got back to business. He forced his victim to strip, then he bound her with a snare wire.

Fearing for her life, Christie began to scream. Her captor's threats didn't shut her up; they made her more hysterical.

Worried that someone would hear the screams and call the police, Hansen jumped out of the back of the camper and into the cab to drive out to the wilderness. As he maneuvered the pickup through the streets of Anchorage to get to Glenn Highway, Christie managed to squirm out of her bonds. Now, besides screaming, she was pounding on the camper walls.

It was getting to be too much for Hansen; things were getting out of hand! He slammed on the brakes, causing his captive to fall forward and bash her head on the camper wall.

Hansen got out and ran around to the back of the camper. Christie had locked the camper door!

Meanwhile, she crawled through the sliding glass window between the camper and the cab and locked the cab doors. But the driver's window was rolled partway down, and Hansen ran up and stuck his arm through to pull up the lock.

As fast as she could, Christie cranked the window up, trapping Robert's arm.

Filled with rage, with a tremendous jerk Hansen freed his arm by breaking the window. Then he yanked his naked victim out of the cab and threw her on the ground.

Hayes bounced to her feet and ran down the street, determined to survive.

Hansen tried going after her, but gave up after a couple of blocks. He went back to his camper, threw Christie's clothes on the ground, and drove off.

Naked, and holding her badly bruised face, Christie Hayes kept running and screaming for help. She reported the assault to police, but wasn't able to identify her assailant from mug shots or provide them with any leads.

That same month, Hansen picked up a sixteen-year-old girl outside the Fourth Avenue Movie Theatre and drove her out to the wilderness with the intention to rape her. But when his captive told him she was homeless and hadn't eaten for two days, he let her go without assaulting her.

Later that fall, however, things turned out differently. Hansen cut a deal for sex with a young woman who would come to be called "Eklutna Annie," thought to have come to Anchorage from Kodiak Island. She was wearing blue jeans, a sweater, brown leather jacket, and high-heeled, red calf-length zip-up boots when she got into his gold camper.

Hansen recalled:

I can't remember if she was a prostitute or dancer. I picked her up downtown and told her I was going to take her to my home. I was heading up to Eklutna Road, there are several offshoot roads there.

I did quite a bit of bear hunting in the area, I built four bear stands [a tree platform from which to watch or shoot bears] in the vicinity.

Hunting bear is a dangerous proposition. With a single powerful swipe of a paw, a bear can maul a hunter, leaving him to stare down at his own entrails hanging out. Sometimes a bear will attempt to decapitate a hunter with its powerful jaws. The prudent way to hunt this dangerous prey, then, is to have it come to you as you wait safely positioned up in a tree.

But today the hunter would keep his feet on the ground.

When it became obvious to the woman that Hansen wasn't driving her to his home, as he said he would, she told him she wanted to go back.

"We're just going a little further," he retorted.

"Well, I'm not," she replied.

He pulled a gun and pointed it at her. "Yes, you are. You do exactly what I say and you won't get hurt."

Continuing north on Glenn Highway toward the Knik River, he turned off onto Eklutna Road, heading east toward Eklutna Lake. Fall rains had combined with the summer runoff from Eklutna Glacier to make the lake's and streams' water levels high, and many of the capillary roads and trails off the main road contained water hazards. The one Robert turned onto did; it quickly became a muddy swamp and he got stuck.

Hansen had a winch on his truck. He convinced his captive to help him use it to get the pickup out of the mud. He drove while she was outside working with the cable off the winch.

It took a while, an inch-by-winch process, but they finally got the vehicle unstuck. Hansen was driving back to pick the woman up when she started to move away into the woods.

He yelled to her to stay put, but she started running. He slammed the engine off and got out and ran after her.

Catching up with her, he grabbed the terrified woman by the hair. In the struggle, she reached into her purse and pulled out a big, black-handled Buck knife. She swung it toward Hansen, but he grabbed the hand that the knife was in and tripped her to the ground.

Hysterically she pleaded, "Don't kill me! Don't kill me!"

He tried to calm her, saying he wasn't going to kill her. But she kept on screaming back, "You are . . . you are going to kill me!" The woman was right.

His victim was lying facedown on the ground when he plunged the knife into her back. He buried her in a shallow grave in the path of a power line.

Shortly after the Eklutna incident, Robert Hansen was hunting when he ran into someone almost as dangerous to him as a bear.

Christie Hayes had switched her place of employment from the Embers to the Bush Company after the bruise on her face healed. She'd also opted for a new wig.

One night, Hansen sat in the Bush Company nursing a beer. He didn't recognize Christie in her new coiffure, but she recognized his pockmarked face when she looked down from the stage. Livid, she pounced on him, kicking and clawing.

The police were summoned, and questioned the two outside the club. Hayes told them about the assault a couple of months earlier, and said Hansen was her assailant. Hansen countered, saying it was just a dispute with a hooker—"she got mad when I wouldn't play ball when she tried to jack up the price." He told the officers he was a married man and didn't want his family to find out about the incident.

If Hansen had been on a supervised parole, or just merely in the parole system, the allegation probably would have been investigated further. But with no flag on his name in the system, the police saw the situation as a respectable family man's word against a charge from a woman of the streets. After the questioning at the Bush Company, the matter was dropped.

Whether the supervised lithium and therapy program mandated by the Supreme Court would have made an impact on Hansen's behavior, had it been established, remains a question. In all probability he would have at least been a suspect in the missing dancers case earlier on. And an ominous consideration: If Anchorage police officer Gregg Baker hadn't taken the Cindy Paulson case to the

State Troopers in 1983, just how long would Robert Hansen have roamed free to pursue his deadly stalk?

But in the meantime, he continued his violent rampage in a hunting ground that was continually being restocked with new and vulnerable prey.

Chapter 29

By 1959, when Robert F. Kennedy—then counsel to the U.S. Senate Rackets Committee—publicly labeled Frank Colacurcio a racketeer, the Seattle mobster had already accumulated a twenty-year track record of violence and crime. In 1941, when he was twenty-three, Colacurcio was convicted of raping a sixteen-year-old girl, and served less than a year of a two-year sentence. After his release, he and his organization were under constant investigation by federal authorities for strong-arm tactics and skimming in cash intensive operations—jukeboxes, pinball machines, and illegal gambling devices.

In the sixties Colacurcio got into the pornography business, then the bar business, eventually operating topless taverns and clubs.

Frank wasn't a Coppolaesque "dapper don" who delegated all the dirty work. He liked to roll up his sleeves. *Seattle Times* reporter Rick Anderson once gave readers an eyewitness account of "Papa" Frank in action.

It was at one of the Mafia kingpin's Seattle nightclubs, the Firelite on Second Avenue. It started when an impatient customer, queued up in a line outside, kicked the door and shattered the glass.

Anderson saw Colacurcio come out of the club flanked by his bouncer, and in his hand Frank carried a long piece of pipe. He hit the man with it, and the poor fellow sank to the ground as he tried to cling to a parking meter.

The mobster kept hitting the crumpled man—blood spurted all over the place.

The man begged Colacurcio to stop. The victim lost all control of his bodily functions and urinated and defecated in his clothing. He wept.

"Papa" Frank gave the mound of flesh one more smack with the pipe, smirked, and swaggered back into the club.

The Colacurcio topless bar and pornography business was run with an organization of about fifty henchmen—brothers, in-laws, relatives, friends, and associates. Federal investigators determined that the expansion of Colacurcio's topless-bar empire followed a simple plan: offer help to a struggling tavern owner by providing the bar with topless dancers, then take over the club and skim profits to avoid paying taxes.

In the late seventies the Seattle mob shipped pornography, violence, and vulnerable women to Alaska, helping to create the milieu of Anchorage's tenderloin district, which provided serial rapist-killer Robert Hansen with an ideal hunting ground.

In 1978 Norman Adams, known to law-enforcement authorities as a Colacurcio associate, arrived in Anchorage and became an invisible partner in the Wild Cherry. At the same time, Adams established a pornography operation behind the corporate name of John's Inc., and opened the Anchorage Book and Magazine Company. The store offered racks of pornographic books and magazines, including child pornography that depicted children as young as three engaged in sexual acts. Besides the literature, the store offered two-bit peep shows in small, curtained booths.

In 1979 Adams pleaded "no contest" to a misdemeanor child pornography charge in an Anchorage court. Later, in 1983, he'd be indicted by an Anchorage grand jury for selling child pornography, but the charges would be dropped.

Gilbert "Junior" Pauole, Colacurcio's former cellmate at McNeil Island, came to Anchorage in 1979 to replace Stanford Poll as manager of the Wild Cherry and Booby Trap. After his release from McNeil, Pauole had worked in Seattle nightclubs run by Colacurcio, and did some troubleshooting in his native Hawaii at Colacurcio's Waikiki Club. Now Junior's job was to give the Seattle mob's topless bar operation in Alaska a shot in the arm.

Immediately the Booby Trap was split into two clubs—the Alaskan Express and Captain Ahab's. The reorganization created two sets of books, doubling the potential for skimming and creative bookkeeping for Colacurcio henchmen.

Across the street from the Wild Cherry, a club called Moby Dick's refused to employ Talents West dancers. A former Wild Cherry dancer recalled, "I saw doormen from Moby Dick's face off doormen from Ahab's and the Cherry with guns drawn."

On November 4, 1979, Moby Dick's burned to the ground.

The following year a fire bomb was tossed into the Mercedes owned by the operator of a topless club called the Red Garter on Dimond Boulevard. It was rumored to be part of an attempt by the Colacurcio organization to extort $30,000 from the man. Shortly after the incident, the Red Garter was signed over to Dimond Enterprises, a corporate front for the Seattle mob, and the club was renamed the Good Times Lounge. Gilbert Pauole became the manager.

Pauole developed a friendship with his landlord at the Wild Cherry, Neil Mackay, who lived in self-imposed exile in Hawaii while retaining extensive business holdings in Anchorage, where he'd made his fortune. It was a curious friendship between a self-made lawyer/businessman and a small-time hoodlum who was a functional illiterate.

Mackay had moved to Hawaii after his second wife, Muriel Pfeil, was murdered in a car bombing in 1976—the incident occurring after a bitter divorce-custody battle between Mackay and his wife.

Two years after the murder, a dramatic custody battle for Neil's and Muriel's only son, five-year-old Scotty, was waged between Mackay and the Pfeil family. The nationally publicized saga included authorities combing the South Sea islands for young Scotty, after his father had him whisked away "for safe keeping" during the legal proceedings. Mackay prevailed and was granted custody of his son. Though victorious, he remained bitter, and repeatedly contended that the Pfeil family had done him wrong and continued to persecute him.

Neil Mackay sent a copy of one of his son's report cards to Pauole, who hung it up on the wall of his basement office in the boxlike Wild Cherry building. Next to it Pauole hung a note from Mackay that said how proud he was of his son's good grades.

On his trips to Anchorage, Mackay brought Pauole clippings of news stories about Hawaiian crime figures, and Pauole would tell the former Alaskan about the Anchorage scene. For Pauole, however, their relationship would eventually be his undoing.

Meanwhile, above and on the streets outside the walls of Gilbert Pauole's office there was little to be proud of, as violence permeated the Fourth Avenue tenderloin district. Between 1979 and 1983 police would respond 207 times to calls at 122 East Fourth (the Booby Trap—Ahab's and Alaskan Express), and eighty-eight times to the Wild Cherry. And those were only the incidents that were reported to police.

Disputes spawned in the strobe-lit bars frequently were resolved with whatever weapons were available, the violence often spilling into the street or hurting an innocent bystander. In August 1981 a twenty-four-year-old man was shot in the head during an argument about a prostitute in front of the Alaskan Express. In the same month, a dancer was injured by a bullet fired by a drunk who'd gone on a shooting rampage at the Wild Cherry.

Through all the mayhem, the money continued to roll into the bars. Pauole would later testify that a good month for a single club meant a skim of $50,000 to $100,000.

The money flowed down to Seattle, and the dancers flew up to Alaska. Anchorage locksmith Robert Maze made frequent trips to the Sleeping Lady on East Second to change locks on apartment doors as dancers came and went.

Sometimes, in the summer, the young dancers would do hand washing and hang it to dry on the open staircase at the rear of the Sleeping Lady. Looking north down the bluff toward the Alaska Railroad station, they'd catch an occasional glimpse of a train full of happy and excited tourists headed for Denali Park, Mount McKinley, and Fairbanks. Looking south, they'd see where they'd be heading for their next shift—a lurid, violent avenue where they were a commodity. That anticipation prompted more fear than enthusiasm.

Chapter 30

Contrary to popular myth, rape is not the acting out of sexual desire, but rather the violent expression of anger stemming from feelings of helplessness or inadequacy. Ironically, it's because persons have in some way been victimized in their own lives and found themselves helpless to prevent or cope with it, that they become rapists.

Under the misconception that rape stems just from sexual urges, society's knee-jerk solutions for dealing with sex offenders have included castration, execution, and imprisonment. Few rapists have received treatment for their problem while in prison, so consequently most of them have repeated their crimes when they were paroled or released.

Embarrassed because of their own normal sex drive, men have difficulty in dealing with the public issue of rape, and some feminists exacerbate that situation by chanting the denigrating charge: "Every man is a potential rapist!" Public policy could develop more effectively if the problem of rape could be approached by both genders in a more informed manner.

The elements of power and control are implicit in the third-degree sexual assaults perpetrated on clients, patients, students, and parishioners by lawyers, psychiatrists, therapists, doctors, dentists, teachers, and clergy. Those situations already have the victim cast in a subservient role. Usually these assaults occur in the "professional" setting—an office, for instance, the assailant's "power center." Incidents on a movie mogul's "casting couch" or on an "executive suite sofa" can involve similar dynamics, though they don't carry the legal consequences of third-degree assault. In many cases these assailants are incapable of functioning sexually outside of their power centers.

Robert Hansen's power center involved his trophy-laden den and the Alaska wilderness, where he was the *hunter,* in control. He fit the category of what's called a "power rapist"—his violence stemming from feeling inadequate in interpersonal and sexual relationships. To this category of assailant, the rape is a means of reassuring self-identity and sexual adequacy.

Magical thinking—fantasy—may delude the power rapists in their crimes; for instance, thinking their victims find them attractive, or that they really want the sex but won't admit it. But deep down the power rapist is not satisfied by the assault, and will go out again and again "to find the right one."

Subsequent analysis of Hansen's confession would reveal some of the elements of his "magical" thinking.

He didn't start out hating all women or his victims, but rather felt he was falling in love with them. He wanted their friendship—he wanted them to like him. But in his own mind he would classify them as either "good" or "bad" women. The "bad"—prostitutes, for instance—he viewed lower than himself.

And with them it was like a game, and the ball had to be pitched before Robert Hansen could "bat." The woman had to approach him to enable him to play out his fantasy; she had to come out and say, "We could do it, but it's gonna cost you some money." Then she was no longer a "good" girl—she was *fair game*.

But sometimes, when Hansen wasn't satisfied with holding power over a woman's body, or denied that power altogether, he would take control of her life. In May 1980, down in Seward, his deadly "game" continued.

Youthful Joanne Messina had thick, auburn hair. Her five-foot-eight-inch body moved gracefully among the fishermen on the Seward docks, her demeanor not revealing that she was down on her luck and laid off from her job at the cannery. She had straight teeth and a confident smile. She smiled at Robert Hansen, who was on the dock, and he initiated a conversation.

She told him she was camped in the state campgrounds. He invited her to supper, thinking, Gee whiz, maybe I can talk this girl into spending the night with me.

After Hansen and Messina finished their meal at the Harbor View Restaurant, they went out and got into Hansen's camper. Then the woman said something Hansen alleged changed everything:

> She just came right out and said, "You know, I don't have a job . . . we could have a real nice time if you have some money."
>
> It just went from day to night . . . she was a prostitute. Anyway, she propositioned me, and that changed the whole thing.

Joanne Messina had "pitched" the ball, and Robert Hansen pretended to go along with the deal. He drove her in his camper north on the Seward Highway to a spot by the Snow River.

Hansen described what happened there. As he talked about it, his voice rose and he became angrier, as if reliving some of the emotion of the experience.

Messina started yelling at him, saying he'd gotten her out to the wilderness under the pretense he'd give her money, and now he was backing off.

"Take me back to Seward, right now!" she screamed.

"Bullshit!" was Hansen's reply. He stopped the pickup and forced his captive back into the camper. "Hey, bitch, this is as far as it's going . . . as far as the fucking money goes, here's all you're worth!" Hansen threw five dollars in her face. "That's all you're going to get, and if you don't like it, that's too damn bad!"

Messina fought her captor, and managed to scramble outside.

Hansen grabbed a .22 revolver he kept in his camper's closet and jumped out

he door with the pistol. He caught up to his victim and hit her in the head with
it.

Crying, on her knees, Joanne held her head in pain. Then, suddenly bolting
up, she charged her tormentor, clawing at his face and screaming hysterically.

Hansen pulled the trigger twice, killing her.

He dragged her body to a gravel pit nearby and pushed some sand and rock
over it.

Messina had brought her dog with her. Fearing it might lead someone to its
master's grave, Robert shot the dog and threw it into the adjacent woods, along
with Messina's camping gear. He took his Smith & Wesson .22 Magnum revolver
and flung it into the Snow River.

Hansen's aberrant hunt was gaining momentum, and the following month
another woman fell victim to his lethal violence.

Roxanne Easlund had come up from Seattle. In the bars on Fourth Avenue
and at the Budget Motel on Spenard Road where she lived, she was known as
"Karen Baunsgarden." She was petite, blue-eyed, and had brown hair that she
bleached blond.

On June 28, 1980, the twenty-four-year-old Easlund dressed in black leather
pants, a fur-trimmed leather jacket, a sweater, and black leather boots, and went
to meet a date on Northern Lights Boulevard. She disappeared, and four days
later her roommate filed a missing persons report with Anchorage police.

The following month, on July 8, Joanne Messina's remains were discovered by
Seward police at a gravel pit at the fourteen-mile post on the Seward Highway.
The body was half eaten by bears.

Nine days later workmen on the Eklutna power line north of Anchorage
discovered a badly decomposed body buried near a high-line pole. She was petite,
white, and couldn't be identified. The Jane Doe became known as "Eklutna
Annie."

At this point authorities had no suspicions linking the two dead women to each
other, or to the missing Roxanne Easlund.

Robert Hansen had at least one more victim in 1980.

No one would guess that Lisa Futrell was forty-one years old as she walked on
Fourth Avenue carrying her makeup case. Her five-foot-two frame was neatly
dressed in dark corduroy pants, green sweater, light blue down vest, and black
shoes. Her gait was confident. After all, she had come up from Hawaii and was
holding her own as one of more than 200 dancers working the clubs in
Anchorage—most of those dancers being in their early twenties or younger.

On September 6, 1980, the Saturday crowd was gathering in the Great Alaskan
Bush Company at 531 Fifth Avenue when Futrell walked in and was greeted by
her employer and Bush Company owner, Edna Cox. Lisa nodded hello and
headed for the dressing room in the basement.

Downstairs, she got out of her street clothes and hung them in the plywood
locker assigned to her. After putting her purse containing a .25-caliber pistol up
on the shelf, she slipped into her robe.

Lisa greeted the other dancers as they arrived for their shift. The women helped each other with hair, wigs, and rollers, and settled down to do their makeup.

In front of her dressing-table mirror, Futrell carefully affixed eyelashes that would accent her soft blue eyes. She opened her robe and let it drop from her shoulders so she could cream her shaved arms. Next, she stood up and creamed her legs and body.

After slipping into her satin G-string and abbreviated bra, she strapped on high-heeled sandals. Surveying herself in the frame of bright lights surrounding her mirror, the dancer made some adjustments to her lustrous black hair, and touched up her makeup.

Satisfied, Lisa went to find a floor manager for whom she'd do a slow twirl for final inspection.

Upstairs, the evening crowd was building. Young men in military uniform were at what the dancers called the "meat rack"—the seats next to the stage that offered the best view of the dancers. Rounding out the crowd were office workers, businessmen, and laborers—all looking for the same thing, the only difference being the amount of money each could or would spend to get it. A service man nursed a beer, while a businessman paid $100 for a bottle of champagne that cost $1.92 wholesale. Another customer purchased a double scotch for ten dollars.

As Lisa walked across the Astroturf in the darkened room of the main floor, a man offered her some champagne from a bottle he'd just purchased for his table. She flashed an appreciative smile as he poured a glass for her. When he sat the bottle down and turned toward the pulsing strobes to look at the dancer on the stage, Futrell emptied the contents of her glass onto the carpet. Speaking through the loud, pounding music, she thanked the man and moved on.

Lisa wanted to get her first dance over with. The first one of the night was always the hardest. She would think about anything when up on the stage—about cleaning, doing laundry, cooking—and keep her eyes just above the customers. The trick was to create a private world that could ensure survival in the real one.

That night, among the crowd, Robert Hansen sipped a beer as Futrell danced. She finished her shift and disappeared.

Apparently, her .25-caliber pistol hadn't given Lisa the protection she'd needed.

Chapter 31

On February 18, 1981, three dancers from the Wild Cherry—Molly Casey, Michelle Strong, and Maria Schmidt—were reported missing. The next day, Junior Pauole had Robert Maze change the lock on their apartment at the Sleeping Lady so it would be ready for the next dancers.

Anchorage authorities still had no inkling that a sex murderer was prowling the tenderloin district. He struck again in the first month of summer.

Malai Larsen was a dancer who wanted to return to her native Thailand, so she looked for ways to get some extra cash fast. The twenty-eight-year-old, auburn-haired Larsen vanished from downtown Anchorage sometime in June of '81. Her disappearance wasn't reported to Anchorage police until July 10.

Still, there was no acknowledgment from Anchorage authorities that something was going on in the tenderloin district as far as women disappearing. And five months later it happened again.

Sherry Morrow had been a dancer in Anchorage for three years, bouncing from club to club. The Wild Cherry would be her last booking.

Friends described the five-foot-six blonde as a pretty girl, quiet and shy. Her roommate saw her as a lonely, troubled, twenty-three-year-old girl who just wanted to meet the right guy and get married.

"I kept telling her there were only jerks that came into the clubs," her roommate said. "Sherry was gullible, easily talked into anything."

When Sherry was last seen leaving a friend's house around noon on November 17, 1981, she was wearing jeans, a baby-blue ski jacket, a pair of blue moon boots, an arrowhead necklace, and wire-rimmed glasses that framed her blue eyes. She was going to Alice's 210 Café to meet a photographer who was going to pay her $300 for posing nude.

Shortly after meeting his intended victim at the café, Robert Hansen got control. He blindfolded Morrow with Ace bandages, and while she knelt handcuffed and helpless on the floor board of the front seat of his brown Subaru, he drove to the Knik River. Crossing the bridge, he turned left off Glenn Highway, followed a winding road past cultivated potato fields, then went through some brush flats and onto a sandbar along the riverbed.

Hansen got his captive out of the car, but before he could get the handcuffs off her, she started kicking and screaming.

Deciding to let her cool off, Hansen took his .223-caliber Mini-14 out of the trunk and sat down by a tree. But the angry woman pursued him.

When it happened, Hansen said, he was just sitting on his ass and she was standing over him, still kicking and screaming. "I just pointed the Mini-14 up toward her and pulled the trigger."

The killer, with bruises on his legs from being kicked by his victim, took a fold-up spade and dug a shallow grave in the silt and sand.

After rolling Morrow's body into the hole, he removed her arrowhead necklace for a souvenir. Before he covered over the corpse, he bent down, picked up the spent .223 shell casing and tossed it into the grave.

He walked back to his car fondling the necklace. Two weeks later he'd collect another.

On the morning of December 2, Andrea Altiery left her apartment to meet an "older man" for a shopping spree at the Boniface Mall.

Andrea, whose stage name was "Enchantment," danced at the Bush Company, as did her roommate, Royale Delcazza, whose stage name was "Magic." The two women had spent nearly every day together for two years—they were very close.

Magic described Andrea as a kind, quiet twenty-three-year-old woman who everyone loved. She'd been given the nickname "Fish," and a friend had given her a necklace with a fish charm.

The two roommates hadn't been suspicious that an older man, probably wealthy, would want to take Andrea shopping to buy her nice things. She'd put on jeans, a red sweater, her gold chain with the fish charm on it, a pearl ring, and a black leather jacket. After primping her brown hair, she gave Magic a "see you later" hug.

Andrea took a cab to the Boniface Mall and disappeared.

Robert Hansen followed his routine and drove the handcuffed and blindfolded Altiery to the Knik River area. Turning onto a service road off the Palmer Highway, he headed for an isolated spot by the Knik River railroad bridge. He'd raped a woman there the week before, and, according to Hansen, "everything had gone fine and I let her go."

In the car, Hansen fondled Altiery's breasts for a while, then held a .22 Browning automatic pistol to her head and forced her to perform oral sex.

Andrea had very large breasts. Hansen proceeded to fondle them some more, until his captive told him she had to go to the bathroom.

They got out of the car, and Robert laid his gun on the hood. Altiery walked off a ways to go to the bathroom, and her captor did the same, unzipping his pants and starting to urinate.

Suddenly, Hansen heard a noise and pivoted to see Andrea reaching for the pistol on the car. She managed to get her hand on the butt of the revolver before Hansen got to her. He grabbed the gun by the barrel, twisted it out of her hand and threw it back on the hood.

The woman became hysterical and started clawing at the pockmarked face of her assailant, kicking and poking her fingers behind his glasses and into his eyes.

The rapist-killer snatched the gun off the car and shot her.

Hansen got a canvas duffel bag and folding shovel out of his car and filled the bag with gravel from the railroad bed. After lugging the bag out to the middle of the railroad trestle, he went back for Altiery's body. He tied the duffel to the dead woman's neck and pushed it and the body off the bridge and into the Knik.

As he walked back to his car, Hansen fondled the pearl ring and fish charm necklace he'd taken off his victim's body.

Sherry Morrow's and Andrea Altiery's friends and family now pressured authorities to investigate the women's disappearances.

After taking a hard look at the situation, Anchorage police finally sensed a link between what appeared to be a total of seven women vanishing from the tenderloin district over an eighteen-month period, and began an investigation of the missing dancers case.

Meanwhile, as the bodies of his victims piled up, Hansen had put the frosting on his image as a hardworking provider for his family—he opened his own bakery. Leasing a store at Ninth and Ingra, he installed ovens and hired John Henning to build cabinets and counters for the shop.

Hansen had acquired a good chunk of the capital to finance his bakery from a fraudulent insurance claim. On January 6, 1981, he reported to Anchorage police that his home had been burglarized and several hunting trophies stolen.

APD report number 81–1290 listed the missing items: one black bear skin, one wolverine skin, one world-record Dall sheep head, one grizzly skin, and one set of walrus tusks.

Hansen filed a claim with State Farm Mutual, and received $13,000 for the replacement value of the items.

Chapter 32

Having come up with no leads in the missing dancers case, Anchorage police went public and requested anyone with information about the women or their disappearances to please come forward.

Shortly thereafter, in February 1982, the police announced that the three dancers who'd disappeared at the same time from the Sleeping Lady a year earlier had actually been spirited out of Anchorage by a church agency and were living safe and sound in the Pacific Northwest.

The women, feeling trapped and desperate, had gone to the church group for help. They were given tickets and travel money to escape.

Possibly fearing retaliation from the mob, the agency insisted on anonymity, but did release a statement to the press:

> A lot of dancers are really decent girls that just got mixed up in something they didn't intend to . . .
>
> Once they get here, they're locked in. They think they're going to make big money, but they get here and find out fast that the clubs are sucking up all the money, and they're not getting any. . . .

The Anchorage police's list of missing dancers dropped down to four, but something else was getting smaller too—Robert Hansen's hunting ground.

On February 18, 1982, Fourth Avenue started to feel the results of an Alaska Alcohol Beverage Control Board investigation. The Wild Cherry, Alaskan Express, and Captain Ahab's were denied renewals of their liquor licenses, mainly because of recurring violence in and around the clubs. The Wild Cherry was the only one the Colacurcio mob was able to keep open, so Pauole continued to manage it and the Good Times Lounge on Dimond Boulevard.

There was a major bomb scare at the Wild Cherry in February of '82, and two months later there were a lot more guns and motorcycles on Fourth Avenue than usual—Hell's Angels arrived from California to seal an affiliation with Anchorage's Brothers motorcycle gang. But not all the skulduggery in the tenderloin district was violent in a physical sense. In 1982 both male and female workers at several Fourth Avenue bars became so fed up with their payroll situation that they sought legal assistance. Their case would drag on, and few employees ever recovered their "stolen" wages. Consequently, many dancers stayed broke—some resorting to prostitution or other quick-cash propositions that made them vulnerable to the serial killer prowling Fourth Avenue.

Sue Luna came up to Anchorage in May of '82, and disappeared two weeks after her arrival. When Bobbie Morehead filed a missing persons report on her sister, it broke a string of five months of no disappearances being reported in the tenderloin district, and it put the number of dancers reported missing up to five.

A few blocks from downtown, the Hansen Bakery was already firmly established and was doing a booming business. In July of '82 Robert took some of his profits and bought a Super Cub—a Piper Cub airplane with a big engine to allow short takeoffs in the bush. Hansen took off the standard tires it came with, and mounted "tundra tires" in their place. The oversized tires permitted landings on rough terrain and swampy ground. He learned how to use them for shoreline landings, turning the large tires into pontoons by locking the brakes as the aircraft landed in the water, then releasing them as soon as the tires hit the land on shore. For takeoffs he just reversed the procedure.

Hansen began to scout for isolated landing spots around the lakes and rivers of the Mat-Su Valley, particularly the Knik River.

Serial killer Ted Bundy once stated that to the serial murderer "mobility is very important." Hansen's airplane enhanced his ability to quicken and extend distancing himself and his victims from the point where he abducted them, and to access more remote locales in which to complete his crimes.

This is a particular aspect of Robert Hansen's modus operandi that became quickly apparent to John Douglas, the FBI agent who drew up the serial killer profile for the missing dancers case:

> Hansen was able to adapt his fantasy of total domination of his victims in a way he couldn't have done, say for instance, in New York City. There, he would've been limited to the back of a van or something.
>
> In Alaska, he had the tools . . . the aircraft to take his victims to isolated areas where no one was around for miles. He could turn them loose if he wanted to, and hunt them down like wild animals.
>
> I've never seen that in another case.

Ted Bundy used a Volkswagen "Bug" in his deadly murder spree—he removed the backseat to make it easier to transport his handcuffed victims in the tiny car. Robert Hansen removed the rear seat of his Super Cub for that same purpose.

And like Ted Bundy, wearing disguises became a part of Hansen's M.O. As Hansen explained, after stalking women in the same area for over a decade, being recognized became a major concern, so he'd bought and used a few disguises. But according to him: "I could never put them on so they'd look halfway real to me."

Besides altering his appearance, he would play a role—pretending to be a doctor, an oil worker from the North Slope, or maybe a photographer. Hansen apparently fooled Tami Pederson by offering her $300 for a photo session.

In early August 1982 Vern Pederson's and Judy Vigoren's daughter gathered her dance costumes and carefully packed them into her blue suitcase. Tami went to meet a photographer, and disappeared. A little over a month later, very near where Tami Pederson took her last breath, the missing dancers case would begin to take on a new perspective.

September 13, 1982, was a "fast" news day. Princess Grace of Monaco and her seventeen-year-old daughter were injured when their car tumbled into a ravine at Cap d'Ail, France; Grace would die the next day. And out of Bangkok, Thailand, came an Associated Press report that 54,000 bodies had been found in mass graves in Cambodia, putting the number of Cambodians killed during the Khmer Rouge regime (1975–78) near the two million mark.

But out along the Knik River, two moose hunters waited for Alaska State Troopers and not the morning paper.

Sometimes it seems you can't take a few days off and leave your job behind. So it was for two Anchorage police officers, John Daily and Audi Holloway, who the day before had stumbled onto what appeared to be a bone joint sticking out of a sandbar. The protrusion was flanked by a dark blue moon boot on one side, and a blue nylon ski jacket on the other—both half-buried in the sand.

With the dusk taking the light, the two men hadn't been sure what they'd found, but they doubted it was a pile of moose bones. Leaving the find undisturbed, they'd gone back to their camp in some willows for the night, and at the crack of dawn found a cabin with a telephone and contacted the troopers.

Officers from the AST's Criminal Investigations Bureau (CIB) met the pair of hunters on a rugged back road near the river. In the daylight on the sandbar, it was evident that what had been stumbled upon was the shallow grave of a woman. The troopers took the remains to Anchorage for an autopsy, and hopefully an identification.

When Sue Luna's sister, Bobbie Morehead, read about the woman's body found along the Knik, she contacted the troopers. Told the corpse was that of a short, blond woman, Bobbie arranged for her sister's dental records to be sent from Seattle.

Morehead asked the dentist not to let her parents know what was going on; if the body wasn't Susie's, she didn't want them to be any more upset than they already were.

Sue Luna's disappearance had dramatically affected her family. Bobbie and her husband had put down money on a house in Seattle the week Susie vanished. They'd canceled their move and forfeited the contract money; Bobbie wasn't going to leave Alaska with her sister missing.

And down in Seattle, Luna's parents not only faced their own anxiety, they faced the questions of their granddaughter, Elizabeth. They kept telling the sad four-year-old, "Mommy will be home soon." As time passed and her mother didn't return, it was difficult to know what to say to the girl.

Bobbie Morehead recalled her niece started having nightmares. "Little Elizabeth didn't understand what was going on. Eventually, she had to see a psychologist."

The dental records didn't provide an answer for Sue Luna's family, only that the body found wasn't hers. For several days Bobbie Morehead rode her horse along the bank of the Knik River, searching its pebbled shoreline and scrub-brush flats for a clue to her sister's fate.

Eventually the body found by the moose hunters was identified as Sherry Morrow, the dancer from the Wild Cherry missing since November of '81. The autopsy showed she'd been killed by a .223-caliber bullet; a spent shell casing of that caliber and some Ace bandages had been found mingled with her remains.

Now aware of the Anchorage police investigation of the missing dancers, the State Troopers returned to the Knik area and searched to determine if there were any other bodies of missing dancers in the proximity of Morrow's wilderness grave. Not knowing where to look on the vast landscape, they found nothing.

Alaska State Trooper sergeant Lyle Haugsven, one of the CIB officers who'd gone to the Knik and brought back Sherry Morrow's body, was assigned to investigate the Anchorage missing dancers cases. The tall, square-jawed trooper began to work with city police to compile records on possible victims and suspects.

Chapter 33

"There are five pimps that have girls working the area," said the big, black-haired Italian as he steered the unmarked car out of the Anchorage Police Department parking lot. APD Vice detective John Gentile (pronounced "jen-tilly") was taking State Trooper Sergeant Lyle Haugsven on a tour of the tenderloin district.

"It's just a few square blocks," the detective continued, "but a lot goes on . . . a lotta money changes hands."

Like Haugsven, Gentile was a native Minnesotan—John was born in a rural area north of Duluth. Both men had ended up in law enforcement in Alaska, but their usual turfs of patrol were in sharp contrast—Haugsven's thousands of square miles of wilderness versus Gentile's beat compressed into city blocks. Now, the missing dancers case had brought them together in a squad car in downtown Anchorage.

"Not all the women working the streets have pimps . . . the ones that don't are called 'outlaws,'" Gentile said. "But sooner or later they get roughed up and look for the protection of a pimp. Sometimes it's the one who had them beaten . . . to sort of move his recruitment process along."

Haugsven was quiet. John Gentile sensed his passenger wasn't comfortable with the situation.

In the early eighties the Anchorage police headquarters was located on Sixth Avenue between C Street and Barrow, within a few blocks of the tenderloin district. Moments after they left the parking lot, Lyle Haugsven hardly felt he was in Alaska.

The darkness of the streets was broken by flashing light bulbs draped on boxlike, single-story buildings covered by gauche, pastel paint jobs interrupted by cartoon figures of long-legged, almost naked women. Signs advertised dozens of topless, gorgeous dancers, and just in case any passerby couldn't read, there were barkers outside the clubs promising a bevy of beauties inside.

The trooper sergeant couldn't help remembering the circumstances of the first time he'd met Gentile. John was a warehouse foreman on the Alaska pipeline, and Lyle was stationed to patrol Glennallen and the Wrangell Mountains area some 200 miles northeast of Anchorage. That was during the pipeline and oil boom era; now, it seemed, things were generally a bust.

Gentile continued to be the guide.

"We know that some of the dancers do hooking on the side, though the clubs maintain that they try to discourage it.

"If the girls don't take care of business in the john's vehicle, they'll use a hotel."

Haugsven saw women on every corner, some bending down to talk business with passing motorists, others pacing back and forth in revealing miniskirts and swinging their handbags.

"Some of these women you see, Lyle, are really dangerous. They don't plan to deliver anything to their customers—they'll grab his wallet when he gets his pants half down, and if the guy doesn't fall on his face when he tries to stop them, they'll pull a weapon on him.

"But most of the girls, I guess you'd say, deliver, and they're the ones in danger a lot of the time. Guess that's why we're here tonight, huh?"

"Uh-huh." The sergeant was chewing on his lower lip as he responded, staring out the car window. "My God, you read about this stuff and see it in movies, but somehow you don't really think it exists this way. What a hell of a place."

It was a Hell of sorts. John Gentile had a sense of humor and humanity that enabled him to make the best of it.

Labeled "the Greek," though his Mediterranean features came from Italian ancestry, the detective had another nickname: "Father Gentile." Once, when he'd come across a distraught, guilt-ridden heavy drinker staggering along Fourth Avenue, Gentile spent over two hours hearing the man's "confession," after which the confessee walked away smiling.

Buoyed by that success, "Father Gentile" went on to preach to the street people behind the downtown Scandinavian Club. As the story goes, after the "service," several of the "congregation" threw their half-full liquor bottles into the garbage. Apparently, the detective had delivered a powerful sermon.

Now, Gentile stopped the squad car at a stoplight. He noticed a tall black woman at the corner across the intersection. "Uh-oh. Sarah's not supposed to be there."

"What?" asked Haugsven.

"The tall one—over there." He pointed. "She's got an 'area restriction.'"

"What the hell is that?" the sergeant asked.

"Sarah was hauled in on soliciting, then released on condition she wouldn't return to the general area where she was arrested. Technically, we could take her in for being in an area she's restricted from. But basically she's a good kid . . . I'll just move her along and not interrupt your tour."

The light changed, and Gentile drove through the intersection and stopped.

"Sarah!" the detective called out.

The woman stooped, and for an instant it appeared to Haugsven that the tight miniskirt atop her long legs might explode from the strain of her bending down.

Shielding her eyes and squinting, Sarah asked, "Is that you, Gentile?" She was apparently nearsighted and not wearing her glasses.

"Yes, it is. Guess you can't see me, and I don't want to see you in this area when you're on restriction. Better move a few blocks."

"Aw gee, Gentile, a girl's gotta eat." The woman flashed a toothy grin.

"Well, they do serve food at the jail, Sarah," the detective responded. "If you stay here, you'll be eating it for breakfast."

Sarah stood erect and put a hand on her hip. "All right," she sighed. Then suddenly her resignation was swept away by a big smile. "Oh, Gentile, I got it."

What now? Haugsven wondered.

"Listen up," she said. "Here goes . . . Don't drink Coke, don't smoke dope, don't jump rope, don't bullshit with the ol' folk, sit down and write a letter to the Pope, gargle with Scope, take a shower with 'soap onna rope,' and never give up hope!"

Sarah finished with a big grin and flung her arms up in triumphant "Tah-dah."

Gentile laughed. "Congratulations. You got it. So here's another one to work on . . . Be fair, be square, comb your hair, change your underwear, say your prayers, don't swear, and the good Lord will be there."

"That one's easy," Sarah responded.

"Yeah, maybe so. Practice it while you walk yourself away from here. Take care now, Sarah."

"You too, Gentile." The woman's purse swung out on its long strap as she pivoted to walk away.

Sergeant Haugsven could tell by the bobbing and swaying of the woman's head that she was practicing the new rhyme as she walked. He turned to the detective. "My God, John, you even talk like them sometimes, don't you?"

Through a relaxed grin Gentile said, "You gotta take it all in stride. Look around . . . you see things here, a lot of it just show, just pretend bullshit."

The two law officers' eyes met.

"But Lyle, you spend some time here and you'll get to know that despite some of the things you see, a lot of folks here are pretty much like everybody else . . . just plain people."

Over the following months, Gentile's prophecy came true for Lyle Haugsven, and for other State Troopers as well.

Chapter 34

In the first dark days of 1983, a blue and white Super Cub made several trips into the Hawk Lake area north of Anchorage.

Hansen burglarized several cabins on the lake, stealing a variety of firearms, hunting trophies, power equipment, CB radios, cassette players, even a propane gas cylinder. He had to hit full throttle to lift the plane off the frozen lake; the aircraft's heavy loads caused the plane to leave deep ski tracks in the snow.

And he continued his deadly hunt.

Twenty-four-year-old Angela Feddern had grown up in Edmonds, Washington, and found that her path in life led to Anchorage, Alaska. She vanished off Fourth Avenue in February 1983, but she wasn't reported missing until May. Angela left behind a five-year-old daughter in Fairbanks, and a mother in Seattle.

Robert Hansen's violence affected several Seattle residents and families. When Vern Pederson came to Alaska in February of '83, with his ex-wife Judy and her husband Gary Vigoren, it was a trip he'd never forget. While Judy and Gary lined up projects for their steel construction business, he walked the snow-covered sidewalks of the tenderloin district searching for information about his daughter Tami's disappearance or present whereabouts.

Having worked in credit collections, he was experienced in dealing with people at cold contact. Pederson carried five-by-seven photos of Tami, passing them out to persons he talked to and leaving her picture with bartenders and doormen at the clubs.

He was staying in the Anchorage home of a friend who was out of town, so he put the phone number on the back of the photos, but not the address of the house.

Vern perceived the people he encountered on the streets to be hiding behind a facade of feigned confidence: "Those kids, both men and women, their attitude was 'I'm tough, I'm okay . . . I can handle anything.' Or it was, 'Hey, I'm *in* here . . . if anybody can find something out about your daughter, I can.'

"And some tried to be reassuring in their way. They'd say Tami was probably all right, but that maybe she just didn't feel like talking with family . . . she'd make contact again when she felt like it."

It's more than likely that many of those young persons who said that to Vern were describing their own situation. But their words gave him little comfort; neither he nor Judy had heard from Tami for six months, and during that time there had been her birthday and Christmas . . . those family times. No, something was very wrong.

Pederson met with Gilbert Pauole in his low-ceilinged basement office in the Wild Cherry. When the Colacurcio henchman tried to tell him he'd never heard of Tami, Vern angrily told Pauole, "You're a damn liar!"

Before going to see Pauole, Vern Pederson had gone to the Anchorage Police Department, where he was told there was a record of his daughter being a dancer at the Wild Cherry. She'd observed a fight at the club, and had been a cooperative witness for the police. Pauole's name was also in the police report about the incident.

Pauole finally admitted to knowing Tami, and he told her angry father that she'd last danced at Ahab's, a bar that had closed down. "That's all I know," he said.

Shaking as he hurried out of the Wild Cherry, Vern thought to himself that maybe it wasn't smart to call a guy like Pauole a liar. After the heated meeting, Pederson made a point to take different routes home to his friend's house.

Vern got a few phone calls from persons who thought they had some information about Tami. He went to the Spenard Bowling Alley to talk to an ex-biker, and the former Brother gave him some names of persons to check with.

Captain Ahab's had been closed down a few months earlier by the Alcohol Beverage Control Board, but Pederson tracked down its bookkeeper who was living in an Anchorage trailer park and still had the bar's records. Tami's father was able to look at his daughter's final paycheck.

"It was made out to 'Pederson,' " Vern recalled. "But it was endorsed 'Peterson,' and it didn't look like Tami's signature at all."

Someone had forged a signature to get their hands on Tami's last wages.

Judy Vigoren told Vern about her meeting with Alaska State Trooper sergeant Lyle Haugsven, and that he'd told her there were other dancers missing from Anchorage. That news was very upsetting.

Subsequently, Pederson crossed paths with Bobbie Morehead, who was trying to find her sister, Sue Luna, and the two exchanged notes. While neither had specific information to help each other out, there was at least a residual feeling that they weren't alone in their searches.

But the cold, short days and long nights in the harsh street culture of the tenderloin district were taking a heavy toll on Tami Pederson's father. He'd grown up in Minot, North Dakota, but had been around enough to consider himself a worldly person. Nothing in his life, however, had prepared him to consider that someone he loved and cared about could end up in an environment like Anchorage's Fourth Avenue. He was becoming very depressed.

Then Vern received a phone call from a woman who refused to identify herself, but gave him a phone number and said firmly, "Call the guy at that number. If anybody can help you, he can." She hung up.

"This is Frank," the voice answered on Vern's fifth try of the phone number.

Pederson explained why he was calling. "The person said you might know something."

"Sure," replied the voice of "Frank." "Tell you what . . . let's have a meet tonight, at the Wild Cherry, say around midnight? Tell the doorman you're comin' to see me."

Vern agreed to the appointment, but after the phone call he began wondering: midnight at the Wild Cherry . . . The implications of the situation made him think of the scenario of the person in a suspense or horror movie who hears the noise in the cellar and then still goes down the steps to check things out even after the basement light won't come on.

Would it be wise to go to a midnight meeting at the Wild Cherry, where he'd called its manager, Junior Pauole, a liar? Might he walk into that windowless box and just disappear?

He called his ex-wife to let her know where he'd be going that night.

"I'll go with you, Vern," Judy Vigoren said.

"No, Judy. It's no place for you. Look, if you don't hear from me by noon tomorrow, go to the police."

For the next few hours Vern Pederson stewed about many of the things he'd seen in the tenderloin district over the past couple of weeks—doormen wearing brass knuckles and having upper arms as big as thighs, bulges in coats that were most certainly guns, and the harsh, dour faces of men staring at the naked dancers in the noisy bars and at the miniskirted hookers on the streets.

Once in a while he'd think of Tami . . . as a little girl. To think of her as a young woman was just too painful now.

Around midnight Vern made his way across a cold Fourth Avenue to the Wild Cherry. As he approached the doorman, he started fishing in his pocket for the cover charge. "I'm supposed to tell you I'm here to see Frank."

The doorman waved off the bill Pederson was handing him. "Inside, check with the bartender. Got that?"

"Uh-huh," said Vern, not appreciating the guy's half-threatening tone . . . and noticing the bulge on the left side of the man's coat.

The Wild Cherry was packed. It took a few minutes for Pederson to make his way to the bar.

"The doorman said to let you know that I'm here to see Frank," he said to the nearest man working the bar.

The person didn't respond, but walked over to the bartender nearest the cash register, who apparently was his boss. In a moment that burly man came over and said, "So you're here to see Frank . . . what's your name?"

When Vern told him, the man nodded, then stared past him. "See those four guys at the corner table back there?"

Pederson turned, following the man's gaze. "Yeah. Which one is Frank."

"Go over and introduce yourself. You'll find out."

Making his way through the crowd again, Vern felt himself perspiring. As he took off his coat, he observed that his actions were being scrutinized by two of the men at the corner table. At the same time, he became aware of something peculiar—though the bar was jam-packed, three empty tables horseshoed the one he was headed for. He felt the need for a couple of deep breaths.

"Good evening, gentlemen," Vern said with the steadiest voice he could muster. He gave his name and said, "I'm here to see Frank."

There was silence as three of the men gave Vern a close once-over, while the fourth sat relaxed with his eyes focused on a drink glass he was rotating in his hand as it rested on the table.

Abruptly, one of the trio gave a quick nod, and they dispersed to the three empty tables, each man facing away from the corner table.

The one who'd remained seated now looked up and smiled. "I'm Frank. Please . . . sit down."

Recalling that evening over eight years later, Vern described the man he'd met that night to have been in his twenties, height around five-ten, weight about 160 pounds, and with a Latin or Mediterranean look—dark hair and complexion.

That description didn't match any of the five pimps who operated in the tenderloin district at that time. Vice detective John Gentile has suggested it may have been Frank Colacurcio's son, Frank, Jr.

It seems logical that the Colacurcio mob could have been sensitive to some dancer's parent making too many waves. Like Robert Hansen, the Mafia preferred to recruit women who, they thought, didn't have strong ties anywhere. Those girls were easier to control, and more expendable in the eyes of society. A dancer's irate father who'd called Gilbert Pauole a liar may have been seen as a potential threat to the topless bar business—enough to cause a Mafia big shot to become involved to ensure authorities wouldn't become "over concerned" about the situation on Fourth Avenue. What Vern Pederson described about the rest of the meeting seemed to point to that conclusion:

"The guy talked very confidently. He said he knew everyone and everything about the clubs, the streets, and even the bikers—the Brothers. He said he was concerned about all the dancers, and made sure they were okay. He couldn't give me any information about Tami, though.

"Most of what he said came across as an attempt to be manipulative. Very unctuous, a real bullshitter . . . but he did have power.

"After we . . . well, mostly he talked awhile, he said he'd show me around all the clubs.

"We went outside . . . the three other guys followed us. He and I got into a green Toronado that was sitting in a no parking zone with its motor running. It was nice and warm inside.

"The three bodyguards, I guess they were, followed in separate cars.

"At all the clubs we visited, the Bush, Good Times, wherever, we didn't pay a cover. They knew him everyplace. At the Arctic Fox all the bikers—the Brothers —seemed to know who he was.

"More than anything, I think he was trying to impress me, let me know he was somebody, and if he couldn't tell me anything about Tami, then probably nobody else could. A snow job . . . I should go back to Seattle, and he'd have things checked out.

"At about four A.M. we drove south out of downtown Anchorage to a hilly, very upscale residential area. We pulled up at a big, trilevel house that had a lot of expensive cars parked around it. From the outside it looked dark because, as I found out, the windows were all blackened over.

"Inside, it was unbelievable—gambling, prostitution, people using different drugs, every illegal vice you might think of.

"That was the last spot on the tour. We went back downtown. Then I drove home, constantly checking my rearview mirror to see if I was being followed."

It was still dark when Vern got back to his friend's house. He was exhausted.

Going inside, he took off his coat and realized his shirt and sport jacket were soaked with perspiration.

Still apprehensive, he dragged himself about the house checking that every door and window was securely locked.

Tami Pederson's father collapsed into a chair in the living room and slumped forward, resting his elbows on his thighs, thinking about the labyrinth of sex, drugs, loose money, and potential violence he'd just traveled through. The maze had included the tenderloin district for the "unwashed," and the trilevel house with its blackened windows for the "elite."

To consider his daughter in that seemingly inhuman world made it difficult for Vern to breathe. The last little hope had slipped away, and he knew he was never going to see her alive again.

For a moment his thoughts escaped their morbid despair as he remembered a smiling, six-year-old Tami bounding toward him, with the movement in her blond hair echoing the bounce of her gait, and her big blue eyes full of happiness and life.

But the vision faded quickly, and Vern rested his face in his hands and wept.

Chapter 35

In Alaska it's not uncommon to find a cabin or camp broken into, but usually the perpetrator is a bear. While this sort of violation is met with some degree of teeth grinding by the homesteader, the anger is generally tempered by an awareness that, after all, man is an interloper in the bear's territory. The bottom-line annoyance of these break-ins is usually the amount of feces the animal has left behind with the rest of the mess to be cleaned up.

But for someone to violate another's camp or cache, to steal goods a man has packed, carted, or lugged into the wilderness for his survival and comfort, is not just a felony according to law—it is a violation of the code of the Alaskan wilderness!

Anchorage dentist Ward Hulbert was looking forward to getting away from the stress and demands of his practice for a couple of days. On March 2 he made his first trip of the year to his cabin on Hawk Lake, and found it had been burglarized. Ward Hulbert was damn mad!

Near his cabin he found distinctive ski tracks left by an airplane that had landed on the frozen lake. He photographed and measured them, then, with some friends, went to nine airfields located in the Anchorage Bowl and looked at hundreds of ski planes. They found only one aircraft whose skis would track to match the measurements—it was tied down at Merrill Field and belonged to Robert Hansen.

A few decades earlier there would have been a hanging. Now, Hulbert went to the police and filed charges instead. But the ski-track evidence wasn't sufficient to secure any warrants, so the complaint died.

Meanwhile, the missing dancers investigation wasn't faring any better. There were no solid leads with which to narrow down a group of suspects whose number now exceeded thirty. The police were stymied, but the hunter of women wasn't.

Twenty-two-year-old Tereasa Watson worked as a prostitute in California, and did the same in Alaska after she arrived in Anchorage in January 1983. On March 25 she kept a fatal appointment with a john.

Robert Hansen took her to Scenic Lake in his airplane and landed on the ice. The details of what happened there aren't known, but Hansen murdered her.

The snow-covered ground was still frozen, so he couldn't dig a grave. He left Tereasa's body where it fell. By the time it would be recovered just a little over a year later, it would be half-eaten by animals.

In the following month, April, Robert Hansen murdered at least two women. He flew twenty-year-old, blond DeLynn Frey out to the wilderness along the Knik and killed her. Frey's disappearance wasn't reported until after the body of Hansen's other victim that month, Paula Goulding, was found on September 2.

But something was different in Alaska as the fall of 1983 approached. With Anchorage police officer Gregg Baker's determined action having given a focus to a now beefed-up trooper investigation of the missing dancers, a twelve-year scenario had been reversed—*the hunter was now the hunted!*

III

to a killer's lair.

Chapter 36

September 14, 1983

From the top of a hill, the hunter's eyes surveyed the acres of scrub brush and occasional pine trees in front of him.

Suddenly, his brow flinched as he caught a glimpse of a shadowy movement 700 yards away.

His hands intensified their grip on the butt and forearm of his rifle as he shouldered it. The hunter's fingers had dirt under their nails, and the stock of his rifle pushed up against a heavy beard growth.

The man hadn't had a shower or bath for several days, either. His stomach was tired of Spam, beef jerky, and beans, and his leg muscles were fatigued in a dull ache, as were his arms, which held his rifle so he could use its scope to determine the source of the shadowy movement.

As the hunter swung his rifle to the left, something in the scope caught his eye, and a short pan back to the right brought him to what he wanted to see.

Lyle Haugsven's faint smile held admiration for the big bull moose he sighted in the cross hairs. He and his hunting partner were trying to maneuver it to the river three miles ahead. That's where they wanted to bring the animal down.

The moose held several hundred pounds of lean meat fed on a wilderness diet devoid of hormones or additives. Generally, moose meat doesn't have a gamy taste, and many people feel it's as good as beef and more healthful to eat.

If the hunters would be able to bag this moose close to the river, one of their major tasks would be lightened—carting all that meat home.

A dry summer had sent rivers and streams down to a low water line, so their currents were slow. The two men planned to use a raft to barge the moose carcass back to their vehicle, several miles down the river.

Haugsven unshouldered his rifle and looked around for his partner. He spotted him on a ridge to the left, and signaled him the location of the moose.

Moving forward down the hill through the brush, Lyle became aware of an incongruous sound, something like the beating of a tom-tom or the slapping of a beaver tail. It was rapid, and quickly becoming louder.

A Bell Ranger helicopter popped over the ridge where the other hunter had been standing just moments before. A voice on a bullhorn cut through the pattering of the helicopter blade and rotor. "Sergeant Lyle Haugsven," it blared. "Lyle, is that you down there?"

The sergeant gave an affirming wave and nod.

"Hate to have to tell you this, Lyle, but you're wanted back at the trooper station as soon as possible. . . . Can't give you a lift . . . just got a call to assist an evac of some hunters hurt in a landslide."

Haugsven waved them on their way.

The helicopter did a pirouette and vanished back over the ridge.

The hunter sighed as he looked back to where he'd last sighted the moose. "Put on a few more pounds fella, and maybe next year . . ."

Back in Anchorage, State Trooper sergeant Lyle Haugsven found he'd left a moose hunt to jump into a manhunt that had a serial killer as its target, and enough manpower involved to be called a task force. APD officer Gregg Baker had pointed out the trail, and trooper sergeant Glenn Flothe was leading the hunt.

The missing dancers task force had compiled Robert Hansen's court, police, and psychiatric records from Iowa and Minnesota, and Trooper Wayne Von Clasen had traveled Alaska as far away as Juneau to gather information about Hansen—a grim history existing on index cards, dispatch and police reports, and case files and microfilm of the state's District, Superior, and Supreme courts.

Anchorage police officer Baker still wasn't aware of the effect his decision to send the Hansen case to the troopers had had the day he went into the Hansen Bakery early one morning.

"The Paulson case was in the back of my mind," he recalled later with a mischievous smile. "I stopped at Hansen's Bakery to buy some doughnuts for the shift. I had screwed up, wrecked a squad car or something, and was paying my dues with the doughnuts. Bob's bakery was the closest by.

"In his shop there was this picture-frame window or opening to allow the customers to see the bakers at work. Hansen was standing in the middle of it, decorating cupcakes.

"So I ordered the doughnuts, and I was watching Bob while I waited for my order. He became aware that I was there . . . Now, I was just casually observing him work. He must have recognized me, and it made him nervous.

"He held the decorating device in one hand, while he twirled the cupcakes in the other. Once in a while he'd look over at me while he worked, and every time he did that, he'd squirt frosting on his thumb.

"Hansen would lick his thumb off and go on to the next cupcake."

Baker kept thinking about the Cindy Paulson case, and that terrified but gutsy woman he'd met on June 13.

A couple of days later he stopped by the trooper station after his shift to see if anything had been done with the information he left at the security desk last summer.

When Sergeants Flothe and Haugsven found out he was in the station, they asked him into their office. He got a warm welcome; he'd never met them before.

The two sergeants questioned Baker for over two hours, looking for any details or recollections that maybe hadn't made it into the Paulson case reports.

It was clear to Baker that the troopers were going after Hansen—they were going to take it all the way.

Chapter 37

Sunday morning, September 18, Robert Hansen looked at the front page of the *Anchorage Daily News,* where an article reiterated what he'd seen reported on the television news the night before. Above the story was a picture of an airboat that had been used in a massive search for more bodies along the Knik River that Saturday.

Explorer Scouts and student troopers had joined AST officers in the effort; over seventy people had participated. The searchers had the support of the airboat, six bloodhounds, an airplane, and a helicopter as they'd combed the banks and sandbars of the Knik, to no avail.

Hansen got up off the sofa and walked into the kitchen. He returned to the living room with a pair of scissors, and smiled as he clipped out the article to put with his other souvenirs.

At another house in Anchorage, Tami Pederson's mother, Judy Vigoren, was tired and frustrated. She'd participated in the search the day before; now her muscles ached along with her heart. She'd called her former husband, Vern Pederson, and told him nothing had come of the search.

Up in Chugiak, the Sunday paper sat untouched on the coffee table at the Morehead house. Bobbie and her husband had brought their horses to the Knik and joined in the search. Sue Luna's body had not been found, but that gave little comfort to her older sister. Bobbie still had nothing to tell her family in Seattle, particularly Sue's daughter, little Elizabeth.

The Alaska State Troopers had hoped the search along the Knik might yield even more incriminating physical evidence. Since it hadn't, they would have to move with what they had to ferret out their suspect.

Of prime importance was to have a material witness to Robert Hansen abducting women from downtown Anchorage. Cindy Paulson was that person, and she could also establish a rape case against Hansen that would, if murder charges couldn't be put together, at least get him off the streets for a while.

But the troopers hadn't been able to locate Paulson. When Sergeant Haugsven said that Anchorage Vice detective John Gentile would be the guy who could find her if she was in town, Sergeant Flothe sent a request through command to APD that Gentile be assigned to the task. That request indirectly caused things to hit the fan for Anchorage patrolman Gregg Baker.

After it became known around APD that the troopers had reopened the Paulson case, one day a lieutenant in Investigations jumped on Baker big-time about talking to troopers. He chewed out Baker in front of other officers. The message was, he shouldn't have taken the Paulson matter to the troopers.

The next day, Lieutenant Kevin O'Leary of Internal Affairs pulled Baker into an interview room and asked him about the incident of the day before. He told the junior officer he wanted to know, immediately, if anything like that ever happened again.

When O'Leary asked Baker if he wanted to do anything about what had happened the previous day, Baker told him no. He felt it wasn't worth straining his relationship with Investigations any further.

Baker's wife Wanda remembered the morning her husband came home from his shift upset that he'd had to put up with the berating lecture from the lieutenant in Investigations. Several weeks before, the couple had sat at the kitchen table in their Eagle River home, deliberating over whether Baker should take the Paulson case to the troopers, realizing if he did, it could affect his career with his department, maybe even cost him his job.

"From the day of the assault, Gregg was convinced Cindy was telling the truth, and he was sure Hansen was behind the disappearances of the dancers," Mrs. Baker said. "So later, when the choice had to be made, we both agreed he should take the case to the troopers. It was the only thing to do . . . the only right thing."

The decision had given the Bakers some short-term relief, but there was still the specter of some consequences for Gregg down the line, and finally there'd been the tense scene with the senior officer.

"It angered me that my husband had to put up with the abuse from that lieutenant," Wanda Baker said. "He didn't deserve it."

Anchorage police officer John Gentile came through, and brought Cindy Paulson to the troopers. Cindy was an emotional young woman. When told the troopers suspected Hansen of murdering Sherry Morrow and Paula Goulding, and probably other women, she broke down.

Cindy had a mother in Seattle. It was decided she would fly down to Washington to visit her; that would give her time to calm down and get herself together before making a statement. Her ticket requisitioned, officers took their star witness to pick up a few things and escort her to the airport.

In September, throngs of hunters fly back to the lower forty-eight out of Anchorage. As the officers brought Cindy into the airport terminal, she gasped and grabbed their arms. In front of them—at the check-in counters of Northwest, Delta, and United Airlines—the floor was littered with moose antlers, caribou racks, and sheep horns. The hunters were taking their trophies home with them.

After a few days at her mother's, Cindy returned to Anchorage. On September

27 she made a one and a half hour statement about her experience at the hands of kidnapper-rapist Robert Hansen that preceding June. Looking at the FBI fire-arms identification manual, she picked out a .357 Magnum that she said her assailant had pointed at her head.

Sergeant Flothe sequestered Paulson away from the milieu of downtown Anchorage; he didn't want anything to happen to the witness.

Detective John Gentile recalled that Flothe had his hands full trying to keep Cindy Paulson on ice during the rest of the investigation. "She took off once, but we found her staying with some people downtown. She was hard to keep under control, but Flothe managed to pull it off."

Officers began taking statements from the peripheral witnesses in the Paulson case; by now the troopers were confident that the man who'd given Hansen his alibi for June 13, John Henning, would change his tune when under oath and confronted with the corroborating evidence against his friend Bob.

Plans were made to interview Dentist Ward Hulbert and other cabin owners at Hawk Lake about break-ins which, according to APD records, Hansen had been accused of. Also, from Cindy Paulson's and Gregg Baker's description of the content of Hansen's den, troopers suspected that Robert Hansen had committed insurance fraud by alleging his hunting trophies were stolen. The State Farm adjuster and the claims file would have to be tracked down.

But now it was time for Glenn Flothe to utilize his contacts developed during his investigation of the serial killer in Fairbanks.

Chapter 38

"The suspect is probably around forty years of age, a thrill killer who may well be a stutterer. He's probably an upstanding and respected member of the community, a person who was rejected as a youth, and he's most likely of above-average intelligence.

And five will get you ten he's been involved in arson, shoplifting, or both at one time or another."

It was bizarre—a pat answer! But that profile came over the phone to Glenn Flothe from several thousand miles away after he'd spent just a few minutes describing crime scene information in the missing dancers case to an agent at the FBI's Behavioral Science Unit in Quantico, Virginia. It fit Robert Hansen to a T.

Immediately, arrangements were made for Bureau agents to fly to Anchorage to consult on the case. The FBI recommended that Hansen be put under twenty-four-hour surveillance as soon as possible.

FBI agent John Douglas began to emerge as a major figure in violent criminal profiling in 1981, with his contributions to the investigation and conviction of the Atlanta child murderer, Wayne Bertram Williams. Since that time he was—and would continue to be—involved in many other notable serial killer cases, the list of which could figuratively be described as "a litany from Hell." Robert Hansen's name went on that bloodied scroll; the trip to Anchorage coincided with going to Seattle to consult on the Green River killer case.

Douglas was one of the cadre of nine FBI agents labeled "the Mindhunters," who planned, and then in late 1983, implemented the Bureau's Violent Criminal Apprehension Program (VICAP). John Douglas was one of the FBI agents used in a composite that was the basis for the character of agent Jack Crawford in the book and movie, *The Silence of the Lambs*.

Armed with a doctorate in education, the culmination of academic studies in several social science disciplines, Douglas and his colleagues offered state and local law enforcement agencies assistance in solving violent crimes. Accompanying the veteran agent on the Alaska trip was Jim Horn, a young understudy who had just joined the ranks of law enforcement officers whose grim job could offer stress-related problems such as ulcers and skin rashes. Douglas would keel over and almost die from viral encephalitis about a year after his trip to Anchorage for the Hansen case, the incident attributed to job-related stress.

Standard police investigative procedures begin at the scene of a crime, where physical evidence is collected, catalogued, then analyzed to attempt to reconstruct what occurred. The behavioralist, who profiles the perpetrator of a deviant or violent crime, seeks the intangible particles of evidence that are implicit in the scene of a crime—rage, hatred, love, fear, irrationality, self-loathing—to help an investigation focus on appropriate suspects.

The operational definition of a crime scene to a behavioralist expands beyond traditional confines to facts and background information about the victims and all the locations involved in the crime, including the body recovery site when a murder is committed in one location but the corpse is buried in another. All of these variables are assessed by applying the current principles of the behavioral sciences—psychology, sociology, political science, and criminology. For example, if a serial killer is leaving bodies of his victims exposed to be easily found, he may be expressing lack of remorse or a desire to *shock* society.

Profiling is not an exact science, and may never be refined to the point of becoming admissible evidence for prosecuting a suspect, but as an investigative tool it can provide the key to collecting evidence to secure a conviction. The legal precedent for that use was established with the Robert Hansen case.

The Anchorage District Attorney's office was invited to attend and participate in Douglas's review of the missing dancers case at the trooper station.

John Douglas recalled: "The Hansen case was the classic model of a serial killer. The chronology . . . twelve years of violent behavior, with acts of arson and kleptomania early on . . . It's hard to tell how many more years he might've killed."

In preparation for securing search warrants, Douglas wrote an affidavit that included the statement: ". . . serial rapist-killers commonly keep mementos of their acts and kits of tools used to accomplish their crimes. Such items would not likely be destroyed and would be retained for a long time."

The following day, the FBI agents coached the troopers on how to interview their suspect, and where and what to look for when they searched Hansen's property. Finished, Douglas and Horn wished the troopers luck and jumped on a plane for Seattle and the Green River killer case.

The troopers tightened the loose ends on a variety of charges they were going to include in requesting warrants against Hansen: the kidnap and rape of Cindy Paulson, the cabin break-ins at Hawk Lake, the insurance fraud with the hunting trophies, and felony possession of sidearms.

In order to go for it all and aim for evidence that would link Hansen to the disappearances and murders of the dancers, a local expert was recruited to fortify the FBI affidavit profiling Hansen as a probable serial killer. Fairbanks psychiatrist Dr. Irwin Rothrock, whose twenty-six years of psychiatric practice included testifying in more than 200 Alaska court cases, went on record stating, "Hansen fits the pattern of a person who might be involved in the missing dancers case." Rothrock saw Robert Hansen as "an impulsive actor," reflected in his kleptomania and the arson in his hometown. Also, he saw the suspect as picking victims "he would view as inferior to himself," and that serial killers "are often avid hunters." The clinching statement was: "People who commit such crimes keep mementos of their criminal deeds."

A confident Sergeant Glenn Flothe approached the Anchorage D.A.'s office with a bulging briefcase, looking for assistance in creating the legal document necessary to gain the warrants. The sergeant was told there was no one available to work on it at the present time. A couple of days later he got the same answer again.

The mood at the trooper station wasn't a happy one. No one could understand why, for probably the most critical case under investigation in Alaska at that time, there wasn't at least one Assistant D.A. available to do some crucial paperwork. It was recalled that when the FBI was in town to consult on the Hansen case, the D.A.'s representatives spent only a few minutes at the meetings. "Wonder how they were able to spare all that time?" became the sarcastic mutter around the trooper station.

But sarcasm wasn't going to solve anything. Sergeant Lyle Haugsven described how the impasse was overcome: "The affidavit had to be done right, or down the line we could lose everything. And it had to be done right away, before Hansen could strike again. So Glenn picked up the phone and called a personal friend in Fairbanks, an Assistant D.A."

Sergeant Glenn Flothe played the second trump he'd gained from his Fairbanks tour of duty. He and Assistant District Attorney Pat Doogan had forged a professional and personal relationship while Glenn was assigned as an investigator to the Fairbanks D.A.'s office and Major Crimes Unit. Doogan had no problem with the efficacy of psychoprofiling violent criminals—he, like Glenn Flothe, had seen it work in the Fairbanks serial killer case.

That Friday night, the sergeant picked up his friend at the Anchorage airport and the two men went directly to the trooper station on Tudor Road. The place was virtually decorated with files and records containing part of the history of Robert Hansen's aberrant, violent behavior.

The pair waded through the documents most of the night, getting only a couple of hours of sleep. Then, it was all day Saturday. The two men were back on the job Sunday morning, and worked straight through until six A.M. Monday, only taking breaks to eat the food brought to the station by Flothe's wife, Cheryl. A rough draft of an affidavit was finished just in time for the trooper to get his friend on an early plane to Fairbanks.

An exhausted Assistant District Attorney Pat Doogan arrived on time at his office that Monday, and met the commitments of his own caseload. Ironically, his selfless role in creating a precedent-setting legal document would remain unheralded.

In Washington, D.C., on October 26, 1983, the FBI held a press conference at the Justice Department as part of its strategy to secure congressional funding to establish VICAP, the Violent Criminal Apprehension Program. At the briefing, the news media were given a startling statistic: "An estimated five thousand Americans were murdered by serial killers in 1982, and the majority of those homicides remain unsolved."

Coincidentally, up in Anchorage on the same day of the FBI's press conference, Sergeant Glenn Flothe went before Judge Victor Carlson with a forty-eight page affidavit and secured eight search warrants to be executed against Robert Hansen and his property on the following day.

Some of those "unsolved" serial killings of 1982 were now going to be solved.

Chapter 39

Anchorage police officer Gregg Baker recalled arriving at the trooper station around five on the morning of October 27, 1983. His friend, trooper sergeant Jim Stogsdill, had phoned him the night before to tell him the Hansen case was going to break, and asked him if he'd like to be a spectator to some of the action. He'd appreciated the invitation.

Baker found the station full of nervous troopers who were waiting for Hansen to leave his house and get to his bakery shop. For some reason he was late. Finally, a little after eight A.M. . . .

From their unmarked patrol car parked in the mini-mall at Ninth and Ingra, State Trooper Forrest Bullington and Sergeant Gerald Smith spotted Hansen in his baker's whites getting something out of his car. The officers, dressed in civilian clothes, got out and approached their suspect. "Robert Hansen?"

"Yes?"

Smith and Bullington identified themselves and told him that troopers wanted to talk with him about some cases under investigation. Would he be willing to come to the station and answer a few questions?

The always cooperative Hansen said, "Sure, just let me give my workers some instructions and get my coat."

Meanwhile, Sergeants Glenn Flothe and Darrel Galyan waited at the trooper station to interview the suspect. Their approach to the questioning would be casual and relaxed, but professional. Lieutenant Bob Jent's office, the most comfortable and spacious at the station, was selected as the place for the interview.

But some "Mutt and Jeff" tactics of interrogation were applied to the setting, Flothe explained:

> The FBI had given us pointers on how to stage the room. We put pictures of the crime scenes on the walls—aviation charts and aerial photographs of the graves found along the Knik River. We spread out files on the desk with the names of his wife, friends, and associates on them.
>
> And we put ten-by-twelve-inch photographs of the victims on the desk . . . Sherry Morrow's and Paula Goulding's.

The plan was to put him in the office all by himself for a few minutes, so he'd have time to contemplate all those articles and stew about their implications.

The interview strategy was simple—they'd talk to Hansen about his life. Its chronology would take them through the arson conviction, the kidnapping and assaults in '71, the various other rape allegations, the chain-saw theft in '76, the alleged burglary of Hansen's home and the Hawk Lake cabin thefts, and finally . . . the murders of the dancers.

Flothe and Galyan wouldn't bring up the Paulson case at all because an interview with APD investigator William Dennis had alerted them to the fact that Hansen was represented on that charge by Fred Dewey. That meant if the Paulson case was to be discussed, as the suspect's attorney Dewey would have had to be notified first. Troopers feared that could have put Hansen on his guard, maybe even caused him to flee.

Arriving at the trooper station, Officer Bullington took the suspect to Lieutenant Jent's office. "Make yourself comfortable," said the trooper, "while I go find the sergeants who want to talk to you."

For a moment Robert Hansen's eyes surveyed the room. Then he took in the view provided by the office's large window, where beyond the Chugach mountain range he could see a jagged horizon. When he looked away from the window, other things caught his attention. . . .

A few minutes later Sergeants Galyan and Flothe came in, introduced themselves, and settled down to what would be a five-hour interview. As a precaution, Galyan informed Hansen of his Miranda rights and had him sign a consent form to have the interview recorded.

As Galyan slated the audio tape at trooper headquarters—"It's now 9:01 A.M." —AST sergeant Lyle Haugsven rang the doorbell at 7223 Old Harbor Avenue, while an armada of police cars waited down the street.

A tall, brown-haired woman opened the door and gave the trooper a cautious look.

Haugsven, in civilian clothes, showed her his badge to identify himself and explained the troopers had warrants to search the premises.

With a quiet reserve, Gloria Hansen moved back from the door and said in a steady voice, "Come in."

Stepping inside, the sergeant saw an elderly woman in a rocking chair in the living room, and a small boy on the floor beside her, drawing with crayons. The little fellow was making a card for his grandmother, who was celebrating her birthday that day. A young girl walked into the living room, and some other young faces peeked around a corner.

Mrs. Hansen explained to Haugsven that she was in the middle of a class with some students she was tutoring. She expressed concern about them, her son and daughter, and her mother-in-law in the rocker, who'd become a widow just a few weeks before.

Sensitive to the situation, Lyle hurried outside to tell the contingent of State

Troopers and city police to hold off until he could help Mrs. Hansen get her family and students out of the house.

"I guess I'll never forget the little boy," Lyle Haugsven said. "He went scooting around, trying to help his mom get some things ready to go. . . ."

The children and Robert's mother sequestered at a neighbor's house, Mrs. Hansen returned with the sergeant to her home.

Before the active search began, the exterior and interior of the residence were videotaped, inch by inch. Then, still photographers took pictures of the interior, followed by officers who sketched the location of objects inside the house and garage. Finally, after a grid search of the den for hairs and fibers was completed, the conventional search got started.

Meanwhile, back at the trooper station, Glenn Flothe and Darrel Galyan were attempting to learn more about Robert Hansen. The troopers knew the threads of aberrant behavior that ran through their suspect's life; now, as the interview rambled between Hansen's past, his family, his hunting and sexual habits, a tapestry began to appear—one that he couldn't or just simply refused to see. He did speak freely about his perception of a painful childhood and adolescence, which he thought had created an uncontrollable anger in him.

Hansen admitted he'd pulled a gun on Susan Heppeard in 1971, and that he'd never really suffered any memory blackout in his life. He knew that at this late date he wouldn't face any consequences for those admissions.

He said he'd been picking up dancers and prostitutes since the early seventies, but denied ever forcing them to do anything by putting a gun to their heads. He maintained he became angry when the women tried to raise their prices, but denied ever threatening them.

As far as the Barbara Fields case in '71, he said: "We drove down to the Sun Rise Inn and spent some time there . . . then she wanted an awful lot more money.

"I told her, 'Bullshit!' . . .

"We got back to Anchorage and I gave her the money and let her out, and I guess her dad is a State Trooper or something."

Hansen refused to admit he'd threatened Fields—that he told her he'd harm her baby son and parents—and feigned ignorance about the piece of paper with their names on it which had conveniently disappeared from his wallet while he was being booked for the kidnap-assault.

Several times during the interview Flothe left the room to talk by telephone with Lyle Haugsven.

"Glenn, we found an aviation map behind the headboard of his bed. It has marks by the Knik River . . . there are over a couple of dozen marks all over the chart."

The search of the house uncovered several handguns, and Ace bandages were all over the house and vehicles. Eventually, a .223 Ruger Mini-14 was found under insulation in the house's attic.

Back at the station, the troopers assumed more control of the interview. According to plan, they'd given Robert a free reign to talk about the past. Now it was time to focus on current matters, particularly the missing and murdered dancers.

"What do you use Ace bandages for?" Flothe asked.

"To have if I throw out either knee. I have Ace bandages around my house by the millions." Hansen explained he'd been injured several times playing softball.

"Do you keep them in your airplane too?"

"Sure."

"Where did you purchase your Mini-14?"

"National Guard Armory down by Madrill."

Flothe moved Sherry Morrow's picture in front of Hansen.

"Who's that?" the suspect asked.

"Sherry Morrow," Galyan answered. "She was found in a shallow grave by the Knik River with an Ace bandage around her arms, or anyway, what was left of them. There was a .223 shell casing found in the grave with the remains, and it's from the same gun as the shell casing found in Paula Goulding's grave. Bob, do you see where we're coming from on this?"

"Uh-huh. Yeah."

"Do you know where that puts you, Bob?"

The questions were coming faster, starting to make Hansen squirm. On the defensive, anger crept into his voice: "You're saying it's out of my gun? Bullshit! It's not!"

Galyan could feel the control of the interview had shifted to the interviewers. "Why are you telling us that everybody is wrong, Bob?"

"Well, they're wrong . . . they are."

The officers' questioning followed a looping pattern, going back to specific occurrences to clear up inconsistencies. But Hansen continued to exhibit the typical sociopath's inability to face the writing on the wall or tell the truth.

The troopers confronted him with the facts that for over twelve years several women had made almost identical allegations against him, identifying him and his clothing, and the vehicles and weapons he used in the kidnappings and assaults. But Hansen stuck to his story that the only time he used a weapon was in the Heppeard incident.

"You're not telling the truth, Bob. You're making yourself look worse," Galyan challenged.

"Look, I can't help that. I'm telling you the truth right now. . . ."

Robert continued to stonewall reality with lies.

Then, Flothe spoke. "We felt there was a problem from listening to Dr. McManmon. Perhaps we're wrong, but we think you've spent the morning trying to convince us that there's never been any problem."

Though it no longer mattered in a pragmatic way to corner Hansen, the officers touched on the gnawing fact that he'd been released in 1978 without the supervised parole mandated by the Alaska Supreme Court.

"It's my understanding," Galyan said, "that back then Dr. McManmon prescribed a particular medication . . . as kind of a maintenance program. Did you follow his instructions and take the medication and go along with the therapy?"

"Yeah," Hansen replied.

"And did that extend for some period of time after your incarceration for the chain-saw theft?"

"For a little while . . . no, I take that back. After I was incarcerated, everything stopped."

"Everything?" Galyan leaned toward the suspect to try and establish some eye contact. "Didn't you ever question that for a period of time they said you needed this medication, and then all of a sudden the whole thing just stops? Don't you think that maybe they did you an injustice by just dropping the whole thing . . . didn't you ever wonder about that?"

"No," Hansen answered calmly, "I don't think so." Then he turned defensive. "Look, I know I shouldn't have taken the chain saw, I should have bought the damn thing . . . then there wouldn't have been the problem in the first place!"

Hansen continued to deny reality and acknowledge any aberrant behavior that required psychiatric treatment. And he never did, nor would he ever, express remorse.

By phone Flothe was informed that the searchers had found a disguise kit and several stolen articles, including the inventory of Hansen's insurance claim for his hunting trophies.

Flothe looked at his watch. It was past noon.

Shown Paula Goulding's and Sherry Morrow's pictures again, Hansen denied ever spending time with either. He claimed to have no knowledge of the cabin thefts, and explained that his hunting trophies had miraculously shown up in his backyard . . . Oh, he'd forgotten to tell State Farm and give back the $13,000 claim money.

The disguise kit? He didn't use it . . . it just didn't work for him.

But he had used it. Robert Hansen wasn't going to admit to doing anything.

Gloria Hansen moved about the house, her arms folded in front of her and shoulders drawn up slightly. She'd seen the officers search about everywhere in her home. Earlier she'd observed their meticulous search of the basement, and couldn't understand why they'd scrutinized the bear rug so carefully. But she'd been irritated by a knee-jerk comment made when a few doughnut bags containing cash and bakery receipts were found in the kitchen: "Hell, he must be an embezzler too." She knew her husband did the books and took the money to the bank once a week, but brought the receipts home every day in inconspicuous bakery bags.

Many officers described Mrs. Hansen's demeanor to be one of a woman dumbfounded by what was happening. She appeared to have no idea of the violence her husband had perpetrated. In fact, several times that day, she mentioned how Robert never physically disciplined the kids, and that there'd never been any violence in their home or anything close to it. She did acknowledge some emotional abuse, though.

Walking into her kitchen, Mrs. Hansen glanced at the clock—one P.M. Looking out the window, she recognized Mrs. John Henning talking with police officers.

Jo Ann Henning had been passing by, and stopped to see what was going on. When the situation was explained to her, she told the officers that her husband had confided in her that last summer he'd lied to the police for his friend, Bob Hansen.

"I'd prefer you hear the details from him. He's up at King Salmon . . . I'll give you his phone number and I'll try to get in touch with him myself."

The officers told the woman that if she talked to her husband, she should encourage him to telephone collect if he had something to say.

At noon the next day, John Henning would call Anchorage authorities and tell them he'd "sort of been roped into providing an alibi" for his friend Bob.

At the trooper station, Sergeants Flothe and Galyan continued in their attempt to get Hansen to open up, saying things they hoped might cause their suspect to drop his guard.

"Let's face it," said Galyan, "most of us don't have much respect for prostitutes or hookers . . . like they're beneath the rest of us.

"And, I think society as a whole downgrades these women. And because these girls disappear from a bar or somebody takes them out and dumps them somewhere, the whole world doesn't come to a screeching halt . . . it doesn't mourn the passing of a prostitute that dies, or even care how it happened.

"By the same token, you found that as you were growing up, girls had a certain power over you . . . they had something you wanted, but they dictated when you could see it, when you could touch it, and when you could enjoy it sexually. . . ."

Now, Sergeant Galyan went to the limit in trying to get Hansen to reveal himself.

"It's kind of nice when you get a little older . . . to be able to turn the tables and dominate for a change, isn't it?"

Hansen started to nibble at the bait. "You mean with prostitutes?" he asked.

"Right."

The suspect shifted on his chair. "Well, if you pay for it you can, yeah."

"Where you weren't allowed to play the leading role or make the big decisions when you were in high school," Galyan observed, "now, because you're paying for it, the prostitute can't reject you. As long as you have the greenbacks, she has to do whatever you want."

Galyan got up, and in the silence, circled the room and sat down again. He continued . . .

"Then comes the time you pull out the gun and the binding instrument—shoelace, wire, chain, handcuffs, whatever. Then, you're in control, and for a change it's you who determines what you get . . . and when you get it.

"Yeah, Bob, I do understand. All those girls, all those years . . . they didn't lie."

But Robert Hansen didn't take the bait, and *he* continued to lie by denying ever kidnapping, raping, or murdering any women.

On the phone again, Lyle Haugsven told Flothe that for all practical purposes the Henning alibi in the Paulson case had been trashed. The .357 Magnum that Hansen had put to Cindy Paulson's head was found, making a total of five handguns in Hansen's possession. Business cards with women's names on them, including DeLynn Frey's, who'd been reported missing just six weeks before, were found in Hansen's garage. And a bag of jewelry was found under insulation in the attic.

Darrel Galyan rubbed his forehead. "Bob, we have a half-dozen cases here that say you stuck a gun to a girl's head and told her if she didn't do exactly what you wanted, you'd kill her. I've been around this business long enough to know that if you do that enough times, something is going to go wrong . . . somebody is going to end up dead.

"And Bob, somebody *is* lying out there dead . . . and everything points at you."

"I never shot anybody," Hansen mumbled.

Galyan slapped the desk and he let some frustration creep into his voice. "You're treating me like some moron sitting here. I like to think I'm smarter than that . . . I believe what those girls said, Bob."

Hansen wiggled on his chair as he said, "I think this is becoming as serious as hell . . . I think I want to talk to an attorney. . . ."

"Sure," Galyan said. "Okay, the time is 1:56. We'll discontinue the tape portion of the interview, as Mr. Hansen has requested an attorney."

Sergeant Flothe put Hansen under arrest, and a warrant was executed against his person:

1. Two vials of blood
2. Urine sample
3. Pubic hair sample
4. Chest hair sample
5. Head hair sample
6. Hair sample—left leg
7. Hair sample—right leg
8. Saliva sample
9. Photograph of person unclothed.

Robert Hansen was locked up, his bail set at $500,000.

Chapter 40

On November 3 an Anchorage grand jury returned four indictments against Robert Hansen: first degree assault and kidnapping, five counts of misconduct in possession of a handgun, theft in the second degree, and theft by deception in insurance fraud. Meanwhile, troopers continued to develop evidence with which to seek formal charges in the missing dancers case.

In the interim between Hansen's arrest and indictment, items in the Anchorage broadcast and print media had given the community its first inkling of whom authorities had caught. Business dropped off at the Hansen Bakery, and up and down Old Harbor Avenue there was shock and disbelief over the news about a neighbor who'd been active in community projects and appeared to be a stable family man. Whatever reality might be, however, most of the neighbors resolved to stand by Mrs. Hansen and her children. Their resolution would never waver.

Robert Hansen went before Judge Ralph E. Moody and pleaded not guilty to all charges. The judge set trial for the week of February 13, and continued bail at a half-million dollars. Hansen's attorney, Fred Dewey, secured a protective order barring official participants in the case from discussing the particulars of the indictments or any uncharged offenses outside of court.

Trooper Wayne Von Clasen recalled, "The order meant we could ask Mrs. Hansen questions, but we couldn't answer any of hers. That made it easier for us . . . but you had to feel for the woman. She just couldn't believe all that was happening to her and her kids."

Troopers had given the District Attorney solid evidence with which to prosecute. Now, as they focused on building a case against Hansen for the murder of the dancers and other victims, the evidence developed quickly.

Seward authorities looked at the aerial map found behind the headboard of Hansen's bed to point out where they'd found Joanne Messina's body in 1980. "Her grave was right here," said a Seward police sergeant, "but there's already a mark."

Also, it had been determined that an asterisk on the aviation chart at Eklutna was at the spot where a Jane Doe, "Eklutna Annie," was discovered in 1980.

Sherry Morrow's and Paula Goulding's graves were also marked on Hansen's map, making a total of four confirmed gravesites of murder victims.

A witness, Brenda Fowler, came forward and identified Robert Hansen as the man she'd seen Sherry Morrow meet at Alice's 210 Café on November 17, 1981.

Lyle Haugsven and Wayne Von Clasen went around to Anchorage jewelers, showing them articles of jewelry found in the search of Hansen's attic. The owner of the Gold and Diamond Company recognized the fish necklace as one he'd custom-made with a charm that was originally a part of a tie pin. He pointed out the tiny hole in the fish where the pin had been mounted. This identification linked Hansen to the disappearance of Andrea ("Fish") Altiery. Additional jewelry items from Hansen's bag of souvenirs were recognized by family and friends of other missing dancers.

The extractor marks on the .223 shell casings found in Morrow's and Goulding's graves matched those produced on shells fired by police in Hansen's Mini-14. Business cards from massage parlors that were found in Hansen's garage contained names or nicknames of some of the missing women.

But at least seventeen marks on Hansen's aviation charts remained unaccounted for, and with winter setting in, the possibility of using the maps to find more bodies was literally "put on ice" until the spring thaw.

So the next step was to wage a little psychological warfare. Information about the evidence developed against Hansen was trickled out to the press.

Given the mass of evidence building against his client, defense attorney Fred Dewey launched a 3-D defense—disassociate, discredit, and disallow. He asked the court to seal documents and close hearings, arguing that Hansen couldn't get a fair trial on the current indictments with a specter of murder charges being discussed in the media and community. Presentation of evidence in open court, Dewey contended, would exacerbate the gossip and necessitate a change of venue.

Assistant D.A. Frank Rothschild countered with an example of his prosecuting a highly publicized murder case labeled a "Spenard Divorce"—a colloquial term that evolved from numerous occurrences of spousal homicides in Spenard during its wild and woolly presuburban heydays of the 1930s and forties, before it became a part of the municipality of Anchorage. A Spenard man killed his wife on Christmas Eve, 1982, and then had tried to burn her body in the fireplace. With the slow news pace of the holidays, the case received extensive media coverage. Nevertheless, Rothchild pointed out, there was no trouble in finding jurors who'd never heard of the case.

Dewey's motion to close hearings and seal documents was declined. So next, he asked for a delay in the trial to allow time for a thorough investigation of Cindy Paulson's background. Dewey argued that her lengthy record of arrests for prostitution in Oregon and California made her a questionable witness. Also, the defense complained that the District Attorney's office was slow in providing documents, and that the volume of material required a considerable amount of time to review when it finally did arrive.

The request for the delay was denied.

．　．　．

Anchorage Daily News reporter Sheila Toomey arranged for an exchange of information with Nick Lamberto, a reporter at the Iowa *Des Moines Register*. Lamberto drove to Pocahontas and researched Hansen's dozen years there, finding that the few people who remembered him recalled a boy going through a troubled childhood. The local newspaper and the courthouse provided articles and records about the bus barn arson and Hansen's subsequent trial.

On January 15, 1984, both the Iowa *Des Moines Register* and the *Anchorage Daily News* ran front-page articles informing readers across their states that a former Iowan was suspected of killing four women in Alaska, and that more than a dozen marks on an aviation map gave a strong implication that the body count could rise.

Hansen read the news in his cell at the Cook Pretrial Facility in downtown Anchorage. He could feel he was being cornered. He told his attorney to try anything to stop or, at least, slow things down.

In Anchorage the next day, Judy Vigoren looked at the calendar. January 16 was her birthday—this one her forty-first. But there'd be no celebrating. She'd read the *Daily News* article about the marks on Robert Hansen's maps, and now she anguished over what it might mean about the fate of her missing daughter, Tami Pederson.

In a last ditch effort, Hansen's attorney, Fred Dewey, attempted to have all the indictments and evidence thrown out of court. He argued the Paulson case was stale, and that the troopers had resurrected the charge as a pretext for searching Hansen's property. Further, he challenged the use of psychoprofiling as the basis for warrants used to seize evidence in the missing dancers case, pointing out that there was no legal precedent for such an application.

The prosecution countered by pointing out that the initial investigation of the Paulson case was severely undermined by the fictitious alibi Hansen arranged with his friend John Henning: "He almost got away with this charade, and now complains police did not discover his fraud sooner."

Superior Court judge Henry Keene ruled the searches were proper, and that all the evidence seized would stand admissible.

Meanwhile, Gloria Hansen wasn't in Anchorage. In order to find some sanctuary for her children, she'd taken them out of school and down for a stay in Arizona.

Robert Hansen asked his friend, John Sumrall, to arrange for the sale of his bakery and airplane. Finding buyers was no problem.

By February, Alaskans are at their peak of "cabin fever," and it's time for them to let off some steam. Starting in 1938, Anchorage began its annual winter celebration called "Rondy," short for "Fur Rendezvous." It coincides with fur buyers coming to Anchorage to deal for Alaska's harvest of furs and animal hides. Through the years the celebration evolved to include a hundred-float parade, dogsled races, parties and dances, and plenty of reindeer sausage, smoked salmon, and scrimshaw (ivory carving) for sale.

During the same time as Rondy, Fort Richardson hosts the military's annual Brim Frost Exercises. Thousands of young soldiers arrive to test their survival skills in the Alaskan wilderness.

With Anchorage bursting with so many outsiders, a large number of prostitutes from the lower forty-eight come up to service the young warriors and the traders of animal hides. So even though it appeared the tenderloin district killer was behind bars, the APD maintained a heavy patrol downtown.

The city was partying and the days were getting longer, but time was running out for Robert Hansen. His attorney had exhausted all strategies to ward off the growing body of evidence against him in the missing dancers case. It was time to try to cut his losses.

On February 17 Fred Dewey had a long talk with his client, and then placed a call to the prosecutor's office. He told Frank Rothschild that Hansen was thinking about changing his pleas, and he might also want to talk about the missing dancers. "He's going to think about it over the weekend," Dewey said.

Chapter 41

On February 22 Anchorage D.A. Victor Krumm, Prosecutor Frank Rothschild, State Trooper sergeants Glenn Flothe and Lyle Haugsven, Robert Hansen and his attorneys all gathered in a conference room downtown. AST lieutenant Bob Jent sat in an adjoining room with equipment to record the meeting. Hansen signed off on his Miranda rights, and his two-day confession began.

The first issue discussed was the defendant's concern to minimize publicity. Both sides agreed to having Hansen's change-of-plea hearing the first thing Monday, rather than letting things drag out to the end of the week.

"I don't care if I have to be brought in three hours before the hearing," Hansen said. "I'd like to avoid being taken across the big parking lot in front of reporters and cameras and such."

"Okay," said Rothschild, "we'll see to it that special transportation is provided . . . we'll do it in a way so you won't have to deal with the press when you enter the building."

The arrangement would work so well that a news photo of serial killer Robert Hansen was never taken; an old picture taken at his arraignment in 1971 was used by newspapers and wire services, with stories about his murders of nude dancers.

In exchange for Hansen's confession, the D.A. guaranteed him that he'd serve his time outside of Alaska, in a federal facility other than the maximum security prison at Marion, Illinois—a harsh, solitary lockup institution.

By lunchtime of the second day, Hansen had confessed to the murders of Sherry Morrow, Paula Goulding, Joanne Messina, the Jane Doe "Eklutna Annie," and a woman whose body he'd thrown off the railroad trestle and into the Knik, who troopers suspected must have been Andrea Altiery—"Fish."

Hansen denied any knowledge of the disappearances of Megan Emerick and Mary K. Thill down in Seward in the early seventies, and said he knew nothing about the death of Celia VanZanten, found frozen to death in December 1971.

However, in addition to the five homicides, the killer admitted raping at least thirty other women over a span of a dozen years in Alaska.

Now Hansen voiced concern about his wife's and children's safety: "Some of my victims were the girlfriends of the Brothers motorcycle gang or sent up here by the Mafia. Something could come down on my family.

"Out of retaliation, my little daughter might disappear and show up three years later when some animal digs her up along the Knik River somewhere . . . my family don't deserve none of that."

Glances were exchanged between the others in the room. But Robert Hansen sat expressionless, apparently oblivious to the piercing irony in the statement he'd just made.

The prosecution agreed to provide whatever security Gloria Hansen and her children might need. Hansen said he was going to urge his wife to move down to the lower forty-eight as soon as possible.

Now the D.A. pressured the killer to open up and come clean: "Your flight charts have over twenty asterisks on them, including places where we found bodies from murders you've confessed to. So we figure there's probably a body at every mark on your maps."

District Attorney Victor Krumm promised Hansen he'd be charged only with the murders he'd already confessed to if he would identify what the other asterisks represented.

"We don't care about all the nuts and bolts of how you maybe killed these other people . . . we're only interested in where the bodies are so that we can recover them.

"So, how many women, sir, have you killed in Alaska?"

"Now, you've got to realize," Hansen replied, "that it's been a long time. I'm going to come as close as I can—"

Flothe interjected, "Let's just do everything with the maps, and then from there we can narrow it down with aerial photographs or enlarged maps."

"Yeah," Hansen said, "I can see this is going to take quite a while. . . ."

The killer identified eleven other gravesites, but even on the enlarged maps, each asterisk represented nearly ten square miles. Things would have to be narrowed down.

On Saturday, February 25, Robert Hansen accompanied troopers to the Anchorage International Airport, where they boarded a large military-issue helicopter for a grim flight over the Mat-Su Valley and northern Kenai Peninsula.

Landing in areas marked on Hansen's charts, the troopers used surveyor tape and spray paint to indicate gravesites pointed out by their handcuffed prisoner. The last stop was at Summit Lake on the Kenai Peninsula, where the confessed killer pointed out where he murdered a black woman in 1978, just a few weeks after being released from prison with no supervision.

The troopers who escorted Hansen that day had to endure something that they hadn't anticipated, though in hindsight, they could have predicted. Included in the profile of serial killers is their propensity to save mementos or return to the scene of their crimes; each can be a stimulus for the killer to relive the thrill and excitement they had when they committed the crime. It was no surprise that Hansen's aviation chart was behind the headboard of his bed, "within hand's reach."

During the helicopter tour of the gravesites, the killer repeatedly became excited or exhilarated. Handcuffed, Hansen would plough through the chest-high snow while wearing snowshoes, and triumphantly point out a grave of one of his victims. A couple of times he became so excited he dropped to his knees to dig in the snow with his hands, looking wide-eyed and with a smile on his flushed, pockmarked face.

When the copter ride was over, the consensus was that no matter what, Robert Hansen would not be taken to any gravesites again. His behavior had strained the law officers' tolerance to the limit; they'd had to swallow their loathing and disgust.

"We gave him a thrill with that helicopter ride," trooper Wayne Von Clasen recalled with a tight lip. "But it had to be done for the sake of the people that wanted to have their loved ones' remains."

Bobbie Morehead guessed why Sergeant Haugsven was stopping at her house on his way home that day. He told her Hansen had recognized the photograph of her sister, Sue Luna, during his confession, so it was pretty much a certainty that she had been one of his murder victims.

"A hearing is set for Monday afternoon," Lyle said. "If you want to be there, it'd be a good idea to arrive early."

Chapter 42

The State Courthouse in Anchorage stands between Third and Fourth avenues, just a few blocks west of where Robert Hansen had picked up many of his victims.

At three-fifteen P.M. Alaska Time, February 27, 1984, he was brought before Superior Court judge Ralph E. Moody to answer for his crimes.

Troopers Lyle Haugsven and Wayne Von Clasen escorted the prisoner into the crowded courtroom to the defense table, then took their positions as guards for the session. Sergeant Glenn Flothe sat at the prosecutors' table with Victor Krumm and Frank Rothschild.

From their positions at the front of the courtroom, Haugsven and Von Clasen saw many familiar faces in the audience, persons whom they'd interviewed and gotten to know during the investigation of the missing dancers. Now, the friends and relatives of the victims were there not to give answers, but rather, hoping to find them.

"Some of the dancers from the clubs were pretty tough women," Lyle Haugsven recalled. "But they—all of them—were in tears that day."

Anchorage police officer Gregg Baker stood with his friend, trooper sergeant Jim Stogsdill, at the back of the courtroom, and ahead of them down front, Bobbie Morehead sat next to her husband.

During the proceedings, Bobbie's feelings of anger and disgust would intensify for various reasons, particularly because Robert Hansen seemed so at ease and showed no remorse for what he'd done to her sister and all his other victims.

District Attorney Victor Krumm informed the court of the plea agreement: For pleading guilty to four murders and all of the grand jury indictments, and for acknowledging his commission of thirteen other homicides not formally charged against him, the state was agreeing never to charge him with those thirteen murders, or to require him to participate in any further investigations of them. And, he'd serve his sentence outside of the state of Alaska.

Defense attorney Fred Dewey confirmed the agreement to the court; then the charges were read and the guilty pleas entered.

Cindy Paulson ran crying from the courtroom, once again realizing how close to death at the hands of Robert Hansen she'd been.

Assistant District Attorney Frank Rothschild addressed the court:

Before you sits a monster, an extreme aberration of a human being, a man who walked among us for seventeen years serving us doughnuts, Danish, and coffee with a pleasant smile. His family was a prop, he hid behind decency.

This hunter who kept trophies on the wall, now has trophies scattered throughout south-central Alaska. And while he doesn't talk about or admit to it, it's obvious from looking at where things started and where women ended up, he hunted them down. He'd let them run a little bit, then he enjoyed a hunt, just like with his big-game animals. He toyed with them, he got a charge out of it. We don't think for a moment that he's told us the whole story. . . .

Judge Moody asked the defense for a statement.

"My client doesn't wish me to speak, Your Honor," Fred Dewey told the bench.

"Mr. Hansen, do *you* have anything to say before this court pronounces judgment on you?" Moody asked.

Hansen answered crisply, "No sir, I don't."

After a pause, the judge spoke:

There are no words which can adequately describe what we have seen here today, and what the defendant has admitted to . . . I can't think of a bigger indictment of society than what we have here. This gentleman has been known to us for several years. Yet, we've turned him loose several times knowing that he had the potential to kill.

Judge Ralph Moody sentenced Robert Hansen to 461 years plus life, without parole.

The court adjourned at 5:45 P.M.—in just two and a half hours Hansen had been convicted and sentenced for twelve years of violent crimes. The proceedings hadn't revealed that he'd done most of his killing during the time he was supposed to have been on a supervised lithium and psychotherapy program mandated by the Alaska Supreme Court. This information was never revealed to the public, or the victims' survivors.

The spectators filed out of the courtroom. No one was smiling or relaxed.

"Things were left incomplete for me," said Bobbie Morehead. "He wasn't really convicted for murdering Susie."

As Gregg Baker and Jim Stogsdill headed for an elevator, Cindy Paulson caught up to them. She gave Baker a hug and an emotional thank-you for all he'd done.

A reporter noticed the scene and came over to get some comments. The officers said they had to get going, and the pair helped Paulson elude the reporter.

The crowd exited the courthouse under a dark sky, the same darkness through which Judy Vigoren drove to the trooper station very early the following morning.

She was livid. She hadn't known the hearing took place until she saw it on the news a few hours after it was over. During the TV newscast, Judy had seen a picture of her daughter Tami flash across the screen as a reporter talked about the murders Robert Hansen had confessed to.

Judy hadn't gotten a wink of sleep all night. She'd been waiting at the station quite a while by the time the troopers arrived for their shift; her anger had dwindled to exhausted resignation.

The troopers were tired, too. They told Judy that the news report was correct, that Hansen had recognized Tami's picture and had pointed out her gravesite when he confessed. In the spring they would attempt to find her body.

So now, for Judy Vigoren and many others, there was still the anguish of the wait for the recovery and identification of the victims' bodies.

Chapter 43

In the G module at the Cook Inlet Pretrial Facility, Robert Hansen awaited transfer to the maximum security prison at Lewisburg, Pennsylvania. He had a last visit with his family, during which he attempted to talk his wife into leaving Alaska right away.

But Mrs. Hansen decided to stay, and would for two years. Eventually, the tauntings from other children would become too much for her daughter and son, particularly the latter, and that strain forced the move. Before leaving Alaska for the lower forty-eight, she divorced her husband.

While Hansen was still in Anchorage, a twenty-six-year-old woman came to the jail to see him. She gave her name at the front desk and declared her intention.

"I don't know if he's seeing anyone, ma'am," said the duty officer. He called Hansen's cellblock and relayed the woman's name.

"I see." The officer put down the receiver. "Ma'am, he said he doesn't recognize your name, and he doesn't want to see visitors anyway. Sorry."

Stoically, the woman turned and walked to the entrance.

The man at the desk watched her go out the door, wondering what she had on her mind anyway—why would she want to talk to a guy like that?

Two months later, *Anchorage Daily News* readers would come to know her by the name of "Leila." In 1974, when she was sixteen years old, on a September night when the northern lights illuminated the Alaskan skies, she'd been raped by Robert Hansen. Almost a decade later, still haunted by the memory of the assault, she'd tell her story to reporter Sheila Toomey.

While Hansen was still in Alaska, the chief classification officer for the Alaska Division of Corrections announced that the expense of renting space for him in a federal prison was going to cost the state about a half-million dollars if the convicted serial killer lived to be seventy-five years old.

Also, in a newspaper article, Pope and Young officials were quoted as saying that Robert Hansen would keep all of his big-game records because "his crimes were an issue apart from his accomplishments as a bow hunter."

However, down the line there would be a change of heart. When the third edition of the *Bowhunting Big Game Records of North America* would be published in 1987, Robert Hansen's trophies and name would be expunged from all the categories of Pope and Young records in which they'd previously appeared.

Finally, on April 10, Alaska's notorious serial rapist-killer was whisked out of the state on a flight to Reno, Oklahoma, the processing center for intake into the federal penal system. Sergeant Glenn Flothe and Lieutenant Bob Jent escorted the prisoner, hoping that during the trip Hansen might tell them about other missing victims and unsolved murders.

But that wasn't to be. "The book is closed . . . I can't see anything in it for me," was the way Hansen brushed off their questions.

With the prisoner headed for Lewisburg, Jent and Flothe boarded their plane for the flight back to Anchorage, thinking about what was ahead. Now, one major task remained to be completed—the grim job of recovering the remains of Hansen's murder victims.

Chapter 44

As the sun rose over snow-capped mountains, ashen fingers of fog slowly retreated from the pebbled flood plain along the Knik River.

In a scrub-brush thicket, a contingent of veteran Alaska State Troopers worked their shovels in the clay-veined soil where the springtime track of the sun had thawed the ground. Each scoop of dirt was laced with glacial silt recently liberated from thousands of years of entombment in ice.

April 24, 1984, the first day of the search for the bodies of Robert Hansen's victims, troopers were worried that he had "taken them for a ride" on the helicopter trip over the Mat-Su Valley. Maybe he hadn't really shown them gravesites.

Glenn Flothe turned shovels of dirt and recalled the flight to Oklahoma. The man who had been handcuffed to his wrist had said he planned to make the most out of his prison life, "doing all I can for Mr. Robert Hansen." He'd told the sergeant that he was going to write a book about his crimes, maybe working up to it by writing humorous short stories first. (Hansen's plan to write a book was based on his assumption that his wife would help him write it. She would flatly refuse to do it.)

Flothe had mentioned the Green River killer to Hansen when their plane made a stop in Seattle. Hansen's reply had been, "You're talking about a guy just like me."

But Robert Hansen had steadfastly refused to reveal anything new during the flight to the lower forty-eight. Just how much had he divulged in his confession?

Two graves were found the first day of the search, so the troopers' fear of having been duped by Hansen was replaced with having to face the haunting trappings of death—a heavy, clinging stench and the frenzied swarms of fat, black flies that stalked the bits of rotting flesh and bones.

Bobbie Morehead's quest to find her sister ended April 27, when she was told Sue Luna's body was one of the two found on the first day of the search:

A reporter called and told me that the troopers had identified Susie's body. She wanted a statement from me . . . I told her I had nothing to say.

A bit later, Sergeant Haugsven drove up to give me the news . . . I didn't tell him about the phone call, and that I already knew.

By the middle of May the troopers had found seven bodies at gravesites Robert Hansen had pointed out to them. The summary went as follows:

On April 24, the victim identified as Sue Luna was located by Jim Creek on the Knik River.

On April 24, a victim identified as Malai Larsen was located in a parking area down from the old Knik bridge on the Knik River.

On April 25, an unidentifiable victim, "Jane Doe," was found lying on top of the ground by Horseshoe Lake in the Mat-Su Valley.

On April 26, the body of Angela Feddern was found on a small lake near Figure Eight Lake, just north of the mouth of the Big Su River. Animal predation had reduced her remains to a piece of jawbone.

On April 29, on an island in the middle of the Knik River approximately one and a half miles down from the old Knik bridge on Glenn Highway, a body identified as Tamara Pederson was located.

On May 9, a victim identified as Lisa Futrell was located buried at the entrance to a gravel pit just south of the old Knik bridge.

On May 17, the body of Tereasa Watson was found, half eaten by animals, at Scenic Lake on the Kenai Peninsula.

With the four victims found before Hansen's sentencing—Joanne Messina, "Eklutna Annie," Sherry Morrow, and Paula Goulding—a total of eleven had been accounted for.

When Judy Vigoren was notified by troopers that her daughter Tami's remains had been identified, she called Vern Pederson. They had their daughter buried in an Anchorage cemetery. Vern flew up to Anchorage and went with troopers to the island where Tami's body had been found. Then he joined them in the search for other bodies—it was a way he could try to cope with his feelings of grief, anger, and helplessness.

In 1923 Anchorage residents dug up stumps to clear a landing strip. When Merrill Field came into existence, the old airstrip became Delaney Park, located between Ninth and Tenth avenues—stretching from P to A streets.

Under a drizzly, gray sky on June 6, 1984, about 200 gathered at the west end of the park for a memorial service for the victims of Robert Hansen. Some of the participants were relatives or friends of the victims, but many were there out of community conscience—to show they cared.

The program for the service was printed on soft-blue stationery, with a quote from Isaiah 49 surrounded by the sketch of a hand forming a gentle hollow:

See, I will not forget you. I have carved you in the palm of my hand.

The memorial service meant a lot to Sue Luna's sister, Bobbie Morehead:

When you've had someone you love missing for a long time, you use up your resources. You go through stages . . . you're mad, you feel alone, you're afraid of relationships. People who cared came together . . . and we weren't alone anymore.

A week after the service was held, Alaska State Troopers used bloodhounds in a last-ditch attempt to find the remaining graves that Robert Hansen had pointed out. The effort was unsuccessful.

In the fall of 1984, and in the summer of '85, heavy rains swept away sand and silt along the Knik.

On August 20, 1985, a pilot testing new tires and practicing landings on a Knik River sandbar discovered the body of DeLynn Frey. She was the last Robert Hansen victim reported missing, and the last one to be found. Tragically, DeLynn was buried in a downtown Anchorage cemetery as a "Jane Doe."

In 1989, while attempting to identify another body, Alaska State Trooper sergeant Wayne Selden went through the Hansen case file and determined that the Jane Doe was actually Frey. He was able to make the identification from a photograph of DeLynn wearing two handmade, silver and tourquoise rings. In '84 DeLynn's mother, Dee Hawks, had told troopers her daughter always wore those rings, and that she had a permanent elbow injury. The rings had been found on the body, and the autopsy report detailed the elbow injury. It took the sergeant several months of paperwork to get Frey's body exhumed.

In April 1990 Dee Hawks picked up her daughter at a post office in Hawaii. The remains arrived in four separate plastic-lined cardboard boxes.

Mrs. Hawks was angry. For six extra years she and her other daughters had pined over not knowing DeLynn's fate.

"I never actually felt she was dead," Mrs. Hawks said. "In the six years she was missing, she was only missing, and we hoped that sooner or later she would show up."

Frey's sisters would think they saw her in a crowd sometimes, and they clung to a fantasy that perhaps their sister was just suffering from amnesia and that sooner or later DeLynn would return home.

The Anchorage mortuary had followed Mrs. Hawks' request to cremate her daughter's remains and mail them to Hawaii. With the grave being almost five years old, the undertaker cremated the whole coffin in order to make sure all of Frey's remains would be in the ashes. So instead of receiving her daughter's remains in one neat little box of ashes as she'd expected, DeLynn arrived literally dismembered into four containers of ashes and dirt.

Dee Hawks filed a negligence suit against the Alaska State Troopers in November 1990: "From 1984 on, they didn't bother calling until five years later. That they would find a body and just throw it in the ground, not even trying to find the people she belonged to . . . I just feel like I'm getting back at them for hurting me."

Chapter 45

After Robert Hansen was put behind bars, his hunting grounds—the tenderloin district—slowly disappeared. The Colacurcio organization lost its foothold in Anchorage. In January 1985 the Alcohol Beverage Control Board closed the Wild Cherry for good; its liquor stocks were removed, and a hand-lettered sign told patrons that the dancers would be performing at the Good Times Lounge on Dimond Boulevard.

In the following months the bar business floundered in a weak economy, and Gilbert Pauole fell into disfavor with his Seattle boss. Then, on November 9, 1985, Pauole and three Anchorage men were arrested and charged with the shooting of Robert Pfeil.

Pfeil was the ex-brother-in-law of Gilbert's friend, Neil Mackay. There'd been bad blood between Pfeil and Mackay since the custody battle for Scotty Mackay, the only son of Neil and Muriel, Pfeil's murdered sister.

An Anchorage police wiretap of a telephone conversation between Mackay and Pauole which sounded as though the two were talking about a murder contract led to Mackay's arrest for the shooting. Pfeil died, so it became murder.

The first court go-round on Mackay's indictment for murder ended in a mistrial when court-disallowed documents mysteriously found their way into the jurors' room. A retrial in February 1988 ended with his acquittal. The defense succeeded in casting doubt on the testimony of Gilbert "Junior" Pauole, "pathological liar."

Pauole had been in the Federal Witness Protection Program since 1986, providing information to the Internal Revenue Service and Justice Department investigations of the Colacurcio mob. Because of this cooperation, Pauole's sentence in prison for his part in arranging the Pfeil killing was only eighteen years, and he could be eligible for parole in 1997.

After his June '88 sentencing, Pauole again disappeared into the protection program. The results of his cooperation with federal authorities soon became evident, as several Mafia figures who'd operated in Anchorage's tenderloin district were put behind bars.

In 1989 Wild Cherry co-owner Norman Adams was sentenced to ten years in prison for tax evasion and conspiracy, and other Colacurcio associates were indicted.

In March 1990 Frank Colacurcio and his son, Frank, Jr., were indicted by a Seattle grand jury for conspiracy and federal tax evasion. U.S. Attorneys brought evidence that the Colacurcios, through corporate nominees Swerland Inc. and Dimond B. Enterprises, had understated the income of the Wild Cherry and the Good Times Lounge in Anchorage during the eighties.

Through plea bargaining, the charges against the Colacurcios were reduced to income tax evasion. Pleading guilty, Frank, Sr., received a thirty-month sentence, and twenty-nine-year-old Frank, Jr., received a three-year sentence—with all but six months suspended.

At the April 12, 1991, sentencing hearing, U.S. District judge John Coughenour granted Frank Colacurcio's request to delay the beginning of his sentence until the fall of 1991. The seventy-four-year-old Colacurcio, whose health was alleged to be deteriorating, wanted to be able to go fishing and enjoy what might be his last summer.

In Anchorage, the Great Alaskan Bush Company on Fifth Avenue did prosper for a while. In fact, owner Edna Cox and her son Jack opened a second Bush Company out by the international airport, and yet another down in Phoenix, Arizona.

Edna Cox was a businesswoman who learned from experience. She installed floor drains at her new Bush companies, so dancers who didn't want to get drunk could save the carpet by surreptitiously dumping their drinks down the drain— sometimes glasses of $300-a-bottle champagne.

Coincidentally, Edna Cox and her son crossed paths with the judge who handled Robert Hansen's release from prison in 1978—Judge James K. Singleton. It happened on July 10, 1984, just three months after Hansen was shipped out of Alaska.

Jack Cox was driving his red Ferrari a little recklessly in downtown Anchorage's afternoon traffic, and Edna was sitting in the passenger seat. Judge Singleton was up ahead in his 1971 Ford pickup. Cox passed Singleton on the right and cut in front of him, causing a collision.

Upset about the dent in his red car, Jack Cox pulled the judge from the pickup, beating him and threatening to kill him.

Cox eventually pleaded "no contest" to assault and battery and reckless driving without a license. He was obliged to pay $1,300 to an Anchorage charity and perform one hundred hours of community service.

Singleton required stitches for some of the injuries he sustained from the assault by Cox, but he healed to go on to better things.

Judge James Fitzgerald, who'd sentenced Robert Hansen in the Susan Heppeard case in 1972, had been appointed to the Federal District Court by Ronald Reagan in 1980. When Fitzgerald retired from the federal bench in '89, President George Bush appointed James K. Singleton to fill that vacancy on October 13, 1989.

A federal judgeship is a lifetime appointment.

Epilogue

1992

The Talents West office continues to operate near Seattle's Sea-Tac Airport, and women seeking their fortunes as dancers can still call its same Seattle phone number that prospective dancers dialed more than seventeen years ago.

Farther north, Anchorage still shows symptoms of a boom and bust pipeline and oil economy. Vacant commercial space is abundant downtown and in the malls scattered throughout the Anchorage Bowl. Residents speculate that another boom might center around cleanup operations from more oil spills like the Exxon Valdez or maybe a pipeline rupture or disaster.

With the turmoil in the Middle East entering into what could aptly be called its third millennium, thus continuing a threat to U.S. oil supplies, some Alaskans are hoping to exploit new oil deposits in their state's national parks.

And, the Yukon Pacific Corporation continues to seek approval of a plan to construct a natural gas pipeline from the North Slope down to Valdez. According to its proposal, in Valdez the natural gas will be liquefied and put on container ships destined for some of the United States' industrial competitors—Korea, Taiwan, and Japan. Walter Hickel resigned from Yukon Pacific in the fall of 1990 to wage a successful campaign for governor of Alaska.

But if there is another boom in Anchorage, chances are there won't be another tenderloin district like Hansen used for his hunting grounds. The Bush Company on Fifth Avenue closed in January 1990; it was the last existing topless bar in which the hunter stalked his prey. As in most areas of the United States, Anchorage's topless bars are no longer concentrated downtown, but are scattered in its suburbs, operating behind the shield of the First Amendment.

The national trend in the topless bar business has gone toward serving only nonalcoholic beverages. This lessens the possibility of official scrutiny that usually comes with a liquor license.

In addition to the table dances like those Robert Hansen paid a few dollars for, dancers now do what are called "couch dances". The customer sits on a couch, usually located in a dark area of the club, and the dancer literally performs on top of him. The customer is not allowed to touch, however. The fees for this service range between twelve and twenty dollars for three minutes. Customers with long attention spans sometimes spend several hundred dollars in an hour.

It has been observed that "a couch dance makes the Lambada look like a polka."

Robert Hansen's hometown of Pocahontas, Iowa, entered the nineties with the remnants of the farm depression that slammed into rural America in the early eighties. The shock and embarrassment of Hansen's crimes had mingled with the more immediate concerns of a bank failure, personal bankruptcies, the effects of agricultural chemicals on the ground water supply, and business failures attested to by vacant commercial buildings.

Finding a parking place on Saturday night has long ceased to be a problem. A statue of the Indian princess Pocahontas stands on the southeast side of town, looking out onto a flat and fertile countryside that holds less than a third of the number of farm families it did when the Hansens baked bread and doughnuts for the community in the fifties.

Robert Hansen is remembered selectively, usually with a comment like: "Oh, you mean the guy who went up to Alaska." Understandably, few care to go beyond that.

But the eighties had provided the town with some fond memories of its sons. With the Catholic school having closed, high schoolers all attended the public school. Consequently, the town enjoyed its first-ever state basketball title in 1987. And three years before that, the year Robert Hansen was sentenced for his violent crimes, the Pocahontas Community High School won its first state football championship.

At the football field on Highway 4 at the southwest corner of the town, a sign proclaims the 1984 football triumph. And next to the stadium stands the bus barn that was built to replace the one Hansen destroyed in 1960—its doors always kept locked.

Barbara Fields, whom Robert Hansen kidnapped and raped in 1971, traded the mountains of Alaska for a mountain range in the lower forty-eight. She owns a big stallion on which she takes long rides in the foothills, sometimes recalling the violent episode on the Kenai Peninsula over twenty years ago:

> The troopers called me in 1983 about maybe going up to testify against Hansen . . . about what he'd done to me.
> When they told me they suspected he'd murdered at least eighteen women, it just numbed me. I went and huddled in a corner . . . I felt I was getting smaller and smaller . . . I broke down.
> I called a friend who'd been raped once, and she hurried over and helped me out.
> . . . I thank God that for some strange reason, I was allowed to live.

Bobbie Morehead and her husband never did move down to Seattle, and still live in Chugiak, Alaska. In 1984, after she'd identified her sister Sue Luna's remains, she had them cremated and sent down to her folks in Washington State.

"But I feel Susie is still up here . . ." Bobbie said. "To me, her grave will always be out there along the Knik."

After the Hansen sentencing in 1984, Alaska State Troopers attempted to help Cindy Paulson stay off the streets. However, she was cited for soliciting for prostitution in Anchorage in 1986, and in San Francisco in '88.

Judy Vigoren, Tami Pederson's mother, lives in Seattle. She and Gary Vigoren are divorced.

"I really think the ordeal over Tami and the stress it made cost Gary and me our marriage."

Vern Pederson, Tami's stepfather, also lives in the Seattle area.

"I've always talked to acquaintances . . . other men who have daughters, about Tami's death," Vern said. "Nothing can bring her back, but maybe her story can benefit some angry kid somewhere."

Dee Hawks, DeLynn Frey's mother, continues to pursue her negligence suit against the Alaska State Troopers.

Glenn Flothe is now a captain, and is the head of the AST's Criminal Investigations Bureau, headquartered in Anchorage.

Trooper sergeant Lyle Haugsven is stationed in Anchorage, assigned to D Detachment, whose patrol jurisdiction is Alaska's west coast. That territory begins 200 miles north of Nome at Kotzebue, and stretches southwest over 1,200 miles ("as the crow flies") to the tip of the Aleutian island chain.

Corporal Wayne Von Clasen is assigned to the Missing Persons Unit in Anchorage. Wayne characterized his experience with the Hansen case this way:

> It became clear to me about a year after the case was wrapped up as best it could be. I was conducting a training in homicide investigation . . . using the Hansen case, as it provides a comprehensive how-to example. I was showing slides, that sort of thing, and I got to the part of the search for all the graves in the wilderness and the recovery of the bodies.
>
> Well, I looked at the screen . . . the pictures of the graves and the decomposed bodies . . . I felt a lump building in my throat . . .
>
> I had to break the session off for a while to get things back together . . .
>
> They were people, a lot of them very young . . . and there were so many.

FBI agent John Douglas, who profiled Hansen as a serial killer, is the program manager of the Bureau's Criminal Investigative Analysis Program of the Behavioral Science Investigative Support Unit in Quantico, Virginia.

Reflecting on the Hansen case in 1991, Douglas said:

> We continue to use the [Flothe] affidavit as a "pony" [a model], sending it out to law enforcement as an example of how to secure warrants using psychoprofiling . . . I remember we sent it to the Green River killer task force.

. . . Hansen may have started killing in his twenties, and is responsible for more murders than we know about. There were probably victims he wasn't proud of . . . ones who weren't prostitutes or perhaps very young. He could be one of our nation's top serial killers.

I'd like to interview him. . . .

After the Hansen case, the Anchorage Police Department made some changes, spent some money on training, and with the avid participation of the District Attorney's office, particularly Steven Branchflower, established a top-notch Homicide Response Team. The operative goal of a unit of this kind is to solve a murder within forty-eight hours after it's reported. Statistically, if a murder investigation goes on for a longer time, the chance of it being solved drops significantly.

Anchorage police officer John Gentile is on medical retirement due to a back problem.

Gregg Baker is now an investigator in APD's Violent Crimes Unit, after a little over four years as a detective in burglary. He recalled:

Working that eleven P.M. to nine A.M. mid-shift in uniform had started to wear me down. I found myself getting short-tempered with people . . . callous, maybe. When that happens, you don't do your job as well. You start missing details and lose your instincts.

In '87, when there was an opening in Burglary, I jumped at it fast. Everyone likes working on this police force, so the only openings and attrition come from deaths or retirements.

As a detective, I work seven A.M. to three P.M. There's a lot to be said for those hours. I'm able to spend more time with my sons Jade and Kaleb . . . they're growing up fast.

In 1990 Robert Hansen was confined at the Lemon Creek Prison in Juneau, Alaska. His stay in Lewisburg in 1984 was a short one; given the nature of his crimes, he wasn't well-received by the prison's population, and for his personal safety he was moved to another institution.

However, for the same reason, he had to be transferred more times. In November of '86, he was installed in an underground maximum security prison in Oak Park Heights, Minnesota, a Minneapolis suburb.

But by 1988 Minnesota's rising crime rate had erased its surplus prison space, so when its contract with the Alaska Department of Corrections expired on May 5, 1988, Robert Hansen was shipped to Juneau. There, at his own request, he was kept under special protective custody.

After a year, he joined the general prison population. He was put to work in a supply room in the basement of the main prison building, and kept under guard at all times.

On January 3, 1990, acting on a tip from an informant, prison officials uncovered evidence of an escape plan hidden in the basement supply-room air duct and among Hansen's belongings in his cell.

Found in the search were a map of southeast Alaska, an aeronautical chart of the Anchorage area, correspondence with a boat broker, articles on aircraft safety and plastic explosives, and a hand-knit winter cap.

Hansen's basic plan was to steal an airplane from the Juneau airport and eventually get to a boat harbor. Two escapes from Lemon Creek in the eighties had failed because the escapees were unable to get out of Juneau. Alaska's capital sits in the shadow of Mount Juneau and Mount Roberts, stretching along a narrow shelf between the Coast Mountains and the sea, and there are no roads out of the city. Hansen's skill as a pilot was to have been the ace up his sleeve for his escape.

But the implications of the articles about plastic explosives and airline safety were ominous. Was Hansen planning to blow up a commercial airliner, perhaps as a vengeful act against a society he perceived as "that monster . . . that did Bob Hansen a personal wrong"—his words to describe his hometown school when he burned down its bus barn in 1960?

After his plan was discovered, Hansen was yanked out of Lemon Creek and locked up in another place familiar to him, the Cook Inlet Pretrial Facility in Anchorage.

Later in the month, he was transferred to the new maximum security prison at Seward and put under administrative segregation—meaning a twenty-one-hour per day solitary lockup.

Prison Superintendent Dan Carothers was quoted as saying Hansen had formulated what he considered to be a well-thought-out escape plan, a thought he'd apparently shared with an unsympathetic inmate.

"Hansen denied the plan when we confronted him with the evidence that was found," Carothers said.

Apparently, Robert Hansen was still up to his old trick of trying to deny the irrefutable truth.

So, if things go according to society's plan for convicted serial rapist-killer Robert Hansen, he will live out the rest of his life locked up near Resurrection Bay, where he used to boat, fish, scuba dive, and hunt; all of what or whom he hunted there may never be known.

Hansen occupies one of the 212 cells at the facility, where he's enclosed by four concrete walls and a steel door. He has a bunk, washbasin, mirror, and there's a toilet at the foot of his bed. A narrow, slitlike window affords him a tantalizing glimpse of the Alaskan wilderness.

Robert Hansen is still viewed as a very dangerous criminal by Alaskan prison authorities.

"What makes him doubly dangerous," said Superintendent Carothers, "is that he's patient."

About the Author

Bernard Du Clos grew up in Pocahontas, Iowa—Robert Hansen's hometown. He first heard about the Hansen case in 1989. Intrigued by its obscurity and by elements that reminded him of Richard Connell's short story "The Most Dangerous Game," he began to look into the case, considering writing a novel. After going to Alaska and beginning serious research into the case, he realized the story should be written as a nonfiction book.